WIRED FOR THE FUTURE

DEVELOPING YOUR LIBRARY TECHNOLOGY PLAN

DIANE MAYO AND SANDRA NELSON

FOR THE
PUBLIC LIBRARY ASSOCIATION

AMERICAN LIBRARY ASSOCIATION

Chicago and London   1999

While extensive effort has gone into ensuring the reliability of information appearing in this book, the publisher makes no warranty, express or implied, on the accuracy or reliability of the information, and does not assume and hereby disclaims any liability to any person for any loss or damage caused by errors or omissions in this publication.

Project editor: Joan A. Grygel

Text design: Dianne M. Rooney

Composition in Stempel Schneidler and Univers using QuarkXpress 3.32 by the dotted i

Printed on 50-pound Victor Offset, a pH-neutral stock, and bound in Bristol 10-point coated cover stock by Victor Graphics

The paper used in this publication meets the minimum requirements of American National Standard for Information Sciences—Permanence of Paper for Printed Library Materials, ANSI Z39.48-1992. ♾

Library of Congress Cataloging-in-Publication Data

Mayo, Diane, 1950–
    Wired for the future : developing your library technology plan /
by Diane Mayo and Sandra Nelson : for the Public Library Association.
      p.   cm.
    Includes index.
    ISBN 0-8389-3491-9
    1. Public libraries—United States—Data processing—Planning.
2. Library information networks—United States—Planning.
I. Nelson, Sandra S.   II. Public Library Association.   III. Title.
Z678.9.A4U6M39   1998
027.473'0285—dc21   98-8814

Copyright © 1999 by the American Library Association. All rights reserved except th[...]
which may be granted by Sections 107 and 108 of the Copyright Revision Act [...]

Printed in the United States of America.

03 02 01 00 99   5 4 3 2 1

Contents

Figures

Foreword

Early in 1997, few libraries had technology plans. Also at that time it was obvious that the Telecommunications Act was going to require libraries to develop such plans in order to qualify for discounts. Moreover, many public library administrators were puzzled about the cost and commitment that technology would require of their organizations. It was in this environment that the Public Library Association executive board, under the leadership of Ginnie Cooper, decided that PLA should lend a hand.

The Board determined that there should be a publication to guide public libraries through the labyrinth of decisions and information gathering that would lead to a technology plan. This plan would need to qualify the library for a telecommunications discount. More importantly, it would have to serve as a road map for that library's plunge into the expensive and uncertain world of technology.

Since the Telecommunications Act was close to being implemented, the PLA board needed to speed up the process of developing this guide. They turned to the PLA Technology in Public Libraries Committee to manage the project. This committee is fortunate to have representatives from a wide range of positions in public libraries of various sizes. All of the members have a strong interest in technology and, in most cases, have had the responsibility of managing technology in their libraries.

Glen Holt of the St. Louis (Missouri) Public Library and Dan Iddings of the Carnegie Library of Pittsburgh (Pennsylvania) were able to quickly develop a request for proposal for a consultant to write this book. Before the announcement was made public, Don Napoli of the St. Joseph County (Indiana) Library, Holly Clark Carroll of the Willoughby-Eastlake (Ohio) Public Library, and Sharon St. Hilaire of the Seekonk (California) Public Library developed criteria that were used to select the consultant. John Blegen of the Glenview (Illinois) Public Library, Laura McCaffery of the Allen County (Indiana) Public Library, Susan Harrison of the New York Public Library, and other committee members reviewed the submittals.

Once Diane Mayo and Sandra Nelson were selected for the project, Sunny Vandermark of the Weston (Massachusetts) Public Library, Dan Walters formerly of the Buffalo & Erie County (New York) Public Library, and others met with the authors to firm up the outline and work plan for the publication. Mary Louise Daneri of the Baltimore County (Maryland) Public Library, Bar-

bara Morland of the Library of Congress, and Martha Knott of the Alamo Area (Texas) Library System also helped review drafts of the publication.

In less than eighteen months, a great number of people worked very hard to make this publication a reality. However, since change is the only constant with technology, the committee has continued to work on this project with the approval of the PLA executive board. A Web site called "Technotes" will be an adjunct to this book. The Web site will cover a variety of technology-related topics with up-to-date information. Through this means, a consistent process can be used in conjunction with accurate and timely information in the development of technology plans.

Wired for the Future: Developing Your Library Technology Plan is part of the growing family of PLA planning publications. The style and approach is familiar to those who have read *Planning for Results: A Public Library Transformation Process.* Thanks to Sandra Nelson's involvement with that project, the tradition of the PLA planning process has been carried forward into *Wired for the Future.* The committee believes that this is a real strength because there is comfort in using a known process when dealing with the rapidly changing environment of technology.

Wired for the Future and the "Technotes" Web site is a further manifestation of PLA's great benefit to all public libraries. Final thanks go to Greta Southard and the staff of PLA for their timely and effective help in making this publication come to life.

—Bill Ptacek
Director, King County (Washington) Library System

Acknowledgments

The authors would like to thank June Garcia, director of the San Antonio Public Library, for her help and support. June gave up a holiday weekend to read the first draft of this book, and her suggestions and insights were, as usual, right on target. *Wired for the Future* is a better product because of June's contributions.

The authors would also like to thank Ruth O'Donnell for her help with the sections of this book addressing the special needs of persons with disabilities. Ruth is a consultant from Florida who is well-known for her work in helping libraries meet the requirements of the Americans with Disabilities Act (ADA).

Introduction

Increasingly, the goal of systems is not to automate, but to enable human collaboration, judgment, and the creation of new value.[1]

The world is in the midst of an information revolution that is comparable in scope and impact to the industrial revolution of the late nineteenth century. It is a revolution in the way information is created, shared, stored, and retrieved. This revolution is based on technologies that will change the distribution of information as profoundly as the development of the printing press did 500 years ago. In the last twenty years these technologies have included the desktop processing power of personal computers, the capture and storage of an astonishing amount of data in machine-readable form, and the development of electronic networks that link users to sources of data, whether those sources are local or remote. These are the tools that support the new flow of information, and these are the tools that have and will continue to have a major impact on public library services.

In 1996 the Benton Foundation published *Buildings, Books, and Bytes: Libraries and Communities in the Digital Age,* a report about libraries and the challenges they face in the digital world.[2] One of the major findings of the report was that

> . . . the public strongly supports libraries and wants them to take a leadership role in providing access to computers and digital information. At the same time, the public voices substantial support for maintaining such traditional library services as book collections and offering reading hours and other programs for children.[3]

However, the report also showed no concurrent support for additional public funding to allow libraries to expand their services. This mixed message will not surprise the library managers, staff, and board members who are responsible for reshaping public libraries in this environment of continuous change.

Libraries are first and foremost places that provide information, and the changes in the way that information is created, published, disseminated, and organized have affected every aspect of the way libraries do business. Collection development, reference services, programs, public relations, staff development, acquisitions, and facility use—the list of library functions that have been affected by technology is comprehensive. The challenge for library managers is to sift through the myriad options available and select those technologies that will enhance the services public libraries provide to their communities. Technology is not and should not be an end in itself. Technology is a powerful tool that allows libraries to provide services and information beyond anything most of us could have imagined ten years ago—*but it is still a tool.*

Why Do You Need a Technology Plan?

Most public libraries have library service plans, many of which were created using planning guidelines published by the Public Library Association (PLA). These plans start by identifying local community needs and then describe the services and programs the library will offer to meet those community needs. Many public libraries also have collection development plans, which focus on creating and maintaining the print and nonprint resources needed to implement the library plan. Far fewer libraries have comprehensive technology plans developed to ensure that the library's technology decisions are made in the context of the library's service priorities as established in the overall library plan.

There are several reasons for this lack of comprehensive technology planning. The first is that the role of technology in public libraries has increased very rapidly in just the past five to ten years. Prior to that, only the largest public libraries needed technology plans, and they normally had full-time staff members responsible for such planning. Second, in small and medium-sized libraries many staff members do not feel that they have the expertise required to develop technology plans. Third, the whole field of information technology is changing so rapidly that library staff feel overwhelmed—they don't know how to plan for a future that is in a state of constant mutation. Finally, there is time, or more accurately, lack of time. Library staff are being swept along in a sea of new and increasingly pervasive technologies, and many have felt like they were always at least two steps behind. Constantly running to catch up is not a mind-set that is conducive to planning.

However, there is evidence that libraries of all sizes are beginning to understand that planning for technology is critical if they are going to continue to provide effective information services to their clients. In addition, libraries are recognizing the need to develop technology plans to manage and coordinate the proliferation of technology applications throughout the library. Some plans are developed specifically to serve as blueprints for the staff to explain how and why technology will be used in the library. Libraries have also developed technology plans to explain to library boards or governing bodies how they are integrating technology into the libraries' operations. Sometimes these plans are also used to justify budget requests to their funding bodies. Other libraries have developed technology plans to ensure that everyone—staff, board members, and funders—has a common understanding of the role of technology in the library and the resources that will be required in the future.

A major impetus for technology planning came with the passage of the Telecommunications Act of 1996, which included the Universal Service Program. Libraries must have approved basic technology plans to qualify to apply for funds under this program. In most states, the state library agency is the body that approves these library technology plans, and many state agencies developed templates for libraries to follow as the libraries developed their plans. However, as libraries completed those templates, they found that it was difficult to make decisions in a void. For many libraries, the development of a limited plan to meet the Universal Service Program requirements underscored the need for a comprehensive technology planning process.

Grant funding, including $400 million available from the Gates Library Foundation and millions more from other sources, is another impetus for planning. Potential donors may be interested in supporting the library's technological infrastructure or specific programs and services that are delivered using technology. For example, the local Lions Club may want to contribute to the resources needed to provide adaptive technology for visually impaired users. A comprehensive technology plan is a key component of any presentation to these potential donors.

Finally, and perhaps most important, as library managers seek to take full advantage of the new technologies, they are realizing that they don't have the information needed to make effective decisions. Technology is affecting every aspect of library operations and every staff member. Without a comprehensive plan in place, staff can become very confused about where the library is going and how they fit into the picture. It is also hard for library managers to explain their needs to their governing boards or funding bodies if, like most libraries, they find themselves preparing budget requests for two years from now. Planning will give library managers, staff, board members, funding bodies, and community members a common understanding of how technology will be used to enhance and expand the services and programs offered by the library.

All of these are good reasons for developing a technology plan, and as you read through the list, you may have decided that you want your plan to do all of these things. However, you will find as you get involved in the planning process that it is impossible to develop a single one-size-fits-all plan. If you are like many other public libraries, the primary reason you are planning is to find ways to manage the growing number of automation applications in your library and to project what your future technological needs will be. You will probably also be interested in developing a document that will serve as a communication tool, but that is of secondary importance to you. If you follow the planning process suggested in *Wired for the Future* with little or no modification, you will develop a plan that will meet the management needs of the library. It will be quite detailed and will include considerable technical information. You may adapt this detailed document to serve other purposes and audiences as well. For example, you might revise it to be less detailed and more descriptive for distribution to public service staff, board members, governing bodies, and the public or, as previously noted, you might use parts of the plan as justification when requesting grant funding.

What Is *Wired for the Future?*

Effective planning requires considerable organization and effort. *Wired for the Future* describes a technology planning process that can be used by any public library. This book is *not* about which technologies a public library should adopt. It does not contain "the answers." This book is designed to help you determine what your options are and then to evaluate and select from among those options the technologies that will best support your library's service objectives. As every librarian knows, technology changes continuously. In 1996 pundits described the evolution of technology in "Internet years": four virtual years for each actual year; by 1997, Internet years were being defined as seven to one. With this pace, there can be no immutable answers, only a continuous process of assessing the environment and incorporating change in an evolutionary manner. *Wired for the Future* is intended to help you establish that process in your library.

In 1998, PLA published *Planning for Results: A Public Library Transformation Process.*[4] This document built upon and expanded the earlier PLA planning documents *The Public Library Mission Statement and Its Imperatives for Service* and *Planning and Role-Setting for Public Libraries.*[5] The *Planning for Results* process includes much that will be of value to public library managers interested in developing plans for technology. After completing the *Planning for Results* process, you will have identified the specific service responses most important to your community. These, in turn, will provide a context for technology planning. You cannot develop a technology plan in a void; you must be able to define your desired outcomes before you can select the tools that will help you achieve them.

Wired for the Future has been divided into five planning steps, each of which is the topic of a separate chapter:

- preparing to plan
- identifying technology needs
- discovering your options
- selecting an infrastructure and identifying products and services
- developing and managing the implementation process

Each chapter includes key concepts, identified as milestones at the beginning of the chapter, that will help planners develop effective technology plans.

To further simplify the planning process, each of the five planning steps has been divided into a group of tasks necessary to accomplish the step. For example, the second step, identifying technology needs, has been divided into three tasks:

> TASK 4
> Review the Library Service Goals, Objectives, and Activities
>
> TASK 5
> Determine Which Activities Require Technology-Based Solutions
>
> TASK 6
> Assess Your Current Conditions

Each task begins with a preview listing the objective of the task, the people involved in the task, the data required to complete the task, the workforms (if any) that have been provided near the end of the book to help planners organize the information needed to accomplish the task more easily, and the approximate time required to complete the task. The tasks themselves are presented in the form of questions and answers. In addition, nine Tech Notes are included near the end of *Wired for the Future* to provide planners with the basic technical information they need to begin their planning. This information includes the definitions for a number of technical terms, which appear as headings or are printed in boldface when they are defined in the Tech Notes. Additional Tech Notes can be found at the PLA Web site http://www.pla.org/technology.

What Will This Planning Process Do for You?

Selecting technology products to use to deliver library services requires that you assess both the technology-based products available and the technical infrastructure (the software, hardware, networks, and telecommunications) needed to deliver those products to your customers. Although you need to begin by identifying the products and services that will help you make progress toward achieving your service goals, identifying the infrastructure you will need to support those products is the key to developing an effective technology plan. Infrastructure investments can be expensive, and for most libraries, it is critical to maximize the benefits received from an infrastructure investment. This leads to a classic chicken-or-egg conflict: Your infrastructure decisions are driven by the types of products and services that best support your goals, and yet the infrastructure(s) you put in place will have a significant impact on the products and services you select. So which comes first?

Wired for the Future will help you resolve this conflict. It will take you through an iterative process that will help you select the products your infrastructure can support and help you build the infrastructure your products and services require.

Carol Tenopir, writing in *Library Journal,* said:

> Just as I assume my electric lights will come on when I flip the
> switch and the telephone dial tone will be there when I want it,

> incredibly complex network connections are becoming routine.
> . . . [Therefore,] many more of us are free to focus on how and
> why patrons and staff use the information on the networks.[6]

The *Wired for the Future* process is about helping you make these "incredibly complex network connections" as routine as possible. It is also about selecting and implementing the technologies that allow your patrons and staff to focus on the incredible amount of information available using the technology.

NOTES

1. Don Tapscott, *Growing Up Digital: The Rise of the Net Generation.* (New York: McGraw-Hill, 1997), 233.

2. Benton Foundation, *Buildings, Books, and Bytes* (Nov. 1996), available: http://www.benton.org/Library/Kellogg/buildings.html (Mar. 1998).

3. Benton Foundation, n.p.

4. Ethel Himmel and William James Wilson, *Planning for Results: A Public Library Transformation Process* (Chicago: ALA, 1998).

5. Public Library Association, Goals, Guidelines, and Standards Committee, *The Public Library Mission Statement and Its Imperative for Service* (Chicago: ALA, 1979); Charles McClure and others, *Planning and Role-Setting for Public Libraries* (Chicago: ALA, 1987).

6. Carol Tenopir, "Taking Online Interaction for Granted." *Library Journal* 122 (Dec. 1997): 39–40.

Chapter 1

Preparing to Plan

MILESTONES

By the time you complete this chapter you should

- know why it is important to design a planning process before you begin to plan

- know what elements to consider when designing a planning process

- understand the skills and knowledge that technology planning committee members should possess

- know what should be included in the orientation you provide to the planning committee

Before You Plan

This library technology planning process is much like the other projects you have managed. There are a number of decisions you need to make before you begin the project that will set the stage for everything that follows. As you have learned in other projects, to make these decisions you first need to have a clear understanding of the overall project. Then, based on that understanding, you will identify your target audience and define the results you expect, decide how you will approach the project and how long it will take, determine how much the project will cost, and select those who will be responsible for completing the project.

The three tasks you need to complete to accomplish the Preparing to Plan step are

TASK 1
Determine Your Planning Process

TASK 2
Select the Technology Planning Committee Members

TASK 3
Provide an Orientation for the Planning Committee

TASK 1
Determine Your Planning Process

This task will set the stage for the rest of your planning efforts. As a part of Task 1, you will decide who will be responsible for each of the sixteen tasks, who else will be involved in each of the tasks, and how long each task will take. You will also determine the resources required to complete the planning process.

Who is responsible for Task 1?
This task is normally completed by the library director.

Who else is involved in Task 1?
The director may choose to involve senior staff in these decisions. The library director will review all of the decisions made during this task with the planning committee chair and the members of the planning committee after they are appointed.

What data is needed for Task 1?

None

What workforms are used in Task 1?

Workform A: Planning Process Worksheet
Workform B: Planning Calendar

What outside assistance would be helpful in Task 1?

None

How long will Task 1 take?

This task should take no more than a week and will be completed before the actual planning process begins.

Why Do You Need to Plan to Plan?

Many people find the concept of "planning to plan" redundant. They start the planning process with a specific deadline or outcome in mind, and they want to get to the "real stuff," or actual planning activities, immediately. However, people who don't take the time to design a planning process at the beginning of their planning efforts often become mired in confusion along the way. That confusion can result from misunderstandings about who is involved in the planning process or what authority those who are involved have. It can also result from an unclear time line or lack of agreement on the use of outside assistance. It will save considerable time and energy if these and other basic issues are decided now rather than later.

What Do You Need to Know to Design Your Planning Process?

Designing the process for your planning efforts is not difficult. The basic process questions you need to answer are

- Who will be responsible for each task?
- Who else will be involved?
- What data, if any, is needed?
- What workforms are used with each task?
- What outside assistance, if any, would be helpful?
- How long will each task take?

As you saw, Task 1 started with these questions, and each question was accompanied by a recommended action. All of the remaining tasks also begin with these questions, and they all include suggested responses for you to consider as you determine the planning process that will work best in your library. As you review the questions and suggested responses at the beginning of each task, you will record your decisions on Workform A: Planning Process Worksheet.

What Special Circumstances Should You Consider When Answering the Process Questions?

Levels of Effort

In some cases, the suggested responses to the process questions will vary depending on the level of effort the library wants or needs to put into the task. There are two levels of effort included in *Wired for the Future:* basic and enhanced.

Tasks completed at the basic level of effort are normally the responsibility of the planning committee chair working with the planning committee and the library staff; they are completed using existing data. The length of time required to complete each task will vary with the task, but the assumption is that most tasks completed at the basic level of effort will take less time than those completed at the second level of effort, the enhanced level. However, don't confuse the level of effort required in your library to complete a task with the quality of the results you will achieve. Many libraries will be able to complete every task at the basic level of effort and end up with comprehensive plans that meet all of their needs.

Generally, a library decides to complete one or more tasks at the enhanced level of effort because of special circumstances in the library or within the technology planning committee. For example, if the planning committee lacks the time or the expertise to complete one or more tasks, responsibility for those tasks may be assigned to a special subcommittee of staff members or to one or more outside consultants. This would be considered an enhanced level of effort. In other tasks, the enhanced level of effort might include more extensive or sophisticated data collection and analysis.

The assumption in *Wired for the Future* is that planners will accomplish each task at the minimum level of effort required to get the task done. All of the process suggestions at the beginning of each task are for the basic level of effort unless otherwise noted. Suggestions for enhanced levels of effort have been included when appropriate and are labeled "enhanced level." These suggestions certainly do not cover all of the process options open to your library. You will want to develop a planning process and time line that work in your situation, using the process suggestions in this manual as a starting point. If you decide to complete a task at an enhanced level of effort, be sure that you have the resources you need and remember that the planning process will probably take longer.

Issues for Complex Agencies

Planning in complex agencies, such as libraries with multiple branches or library systems with a number of members, can present special challenges. However, there is no reason to assume that complex agencies should automatically select the enhanced level of effort every time that option is provided. Certainly, planners in complex agencies will need to ensure that the needs of all units are considered in the planning process. That may or may not require an enhanced level of effort for some tasks. Before planners in complex agencies can make any decisions about what will be required to complete each of the tasks, some basic questions should be answered:

> Will the agency develop a systemwide plan, or will each unit of the system develop a separate plan?
>
> If the agency develops a systemwide plan, what role will the individual units have in implementing the plan?
>
> If the units develop separate plans, how will they be integrated into a systemwide plan, if at all?
>
> How should the staff in the individual units be involved in the planning process?

Once these decisions have been made, the person responsible for designing the planning process can use that information to complete Workform A.

When Should You Consider Using Outside Assistance?

This planning process is designed to be completed at the basic level of effort by library staff and planning committee members without outside assistance. However, as noted previously, there may be occasions when an outside expert or consultant could provide valuable assistance to the planning committee. Two types of outside help might be useful: content help and process help. If you find that the planning committee lacks the information or expertise needed to make a decision, you may want to find an outside expert to inform the committee and to help make the decision. For example, in Task 8: Evaluate the Options for Your Highest Priority Activities, you may need to ask someone from your local phone company to provide the committee with an introduction to the telecommunication options open to the library and to discuss the pros and cons of each. On the other hand, there may be occasions when the committee members have all the information they need but are unable to reach agreement based on that information. In those cases, it may be helpful to ask an outside consultant or facilitator to help the committee reach consensus.

In general, the decisions to use outside help and where to get that help are made based on the resources you have available, the complexity of your planning environment, and the time frame for your planning process. Perhaps the most important resource to consider is the planning committee itself. If the committee chair has strong facilitation skills and the committee members include people with technology and public service expertise, it is less likely that the library will have to use outside assistance. Obviously, another resource issue is the availability of funding to pay for consultant services. Not all outside assistance costs money, but libraries that can afford to do so frequently choose to hire an outside consultant to work with the planning committee to develop the technology plan.

As stated earlier, complex agencies (libraries with multiple outlets and system and regional libraries, etc.) in particular may find that they need outside assistance to manage part or all of their planning processes. If a complex agency decides to include representatives from all of the organization's units in the planning process, coordinating such a multiunit planning effort can be challenging and may be more than the planning chair can manage along with his or her other responsibilities.

Another factor that may indicate that you should consider using outside resources is your planning time line. If you have a short time in which to produce your technology plan, you are more likely to need to hire someone to work with the planning committee. In most instances, the planning committee members are adding their planning responsibilities on top of their regular library duties, and in the case of committee members who are not library staff, their regular jobs. As a result, they cannot devote all of their energies to the planning process, and inevitably, the process takes longer than it would with a paid consultant to work with the committee.

If you decide you do need outside assistance, you then have to find that assistance. How you proceed will be based on the resources you have to pay for the assistance. If, like most public libraries, you have limited resources, you may want to draw from the wide variety of free or very inexpensive technical/expert assistance that is available. Sources of general technical assistance include

  city or county government technical or computer support staff

  local school or school district office technical or computer support staff

  local software or hardware users groups

For library-specific expert assistance, consider these resources:

  state library consultants

  system or regional library consultants

  resource sharing consortia staff members

other library directors in libraries approximately your size

technical or computer support staff in the larger public libraries in your state

local school librarians (if the school library media center has successfully integrated technology into its programs)

local community college or college librarians

support personnel from software vendors

representatives from your automation vendor if you already have an on-line system

Most libraries also have access to a number of local people who will provide free or inexpensive process assistance. They include

college or community college professors

county extension personnel

principals or school superintendents

guidance counselors

clergy

If you have the necessary funds, you may want to hire a specialist in library technology issues or library planning to work with the planning committee. In most cases this will require that you develop and issue a request for proposal (RFP). Your local government probably has a format for RFPs. If not, your state library agency may be able to send you one or two samples from other libraries in the state.

It is sometimes difficult to know how to notify potential consultants that you are ready to issue an RFP. One way is to publish a notice of your RFP in *Library Hotline,* which is read by many consultants. Another is to post notice of your RFP on Publib (www.sunsite.berkeley.edu/publib/) or one of the other library listservs. A number of organizations, including two divisions of the American Library Association (ALA), the Library Information and Technology Association (LITA) and the Association of Specialized and Cooperative Agencies (ASCLA), publish lists of consultants and their specialties. These can be obtained by calling the appropriate organization. The Urban Libraries Council (ULC) also publishes a list of recommended consultants for its members. You might also want to talk to your colleagues in other libraries to see if they can recommend one or more consultants.

How Long Will It Take to Develop the Technology Plan?

As you complete Workform A, you will be asked to estimate the length of time it will take to accomplish each task. Suggested time frames are included at the beginning of each task, but they are, at best, only guidelines. If you choose an enhanced level of effort or have to collect basic data, the task may take longer than the suggested time. Another factor that can affect the planning time is the composition of the planning committee itself. It often takes longer for large committees to reach decisions than it does for smaller committees. Committees in which all of the members have a common understanding of technology and the library's current operations will usually complete their tasks more quickly than committees with members reflecting diverse levels of information and experience. As stated previously, if you choose to hire a person to manage the planning process, you will probably complete the process more quickly than if the committee works on its own because the consultant will spend more-focused time on the project than staff and volunteers can.

After you have completed Workform A, you will use your estimated times to develop Workform B: Planning Calendar. The Planning Calendar is a one-year Gantt chart. To use the workform, mark the starting date for your planning process and then begin to transfer the information on how long each task will take from Workform A. Indicate the start and end date for each task, and connect the two dates with a line.

As you work, consider what else will be happening during the time you are scheduling. For example, if one or more tasks are scheduled to occur in November and December, you may need to adjust the length of time for those tasks due to holiday schedules. Consider other events that may have an impact on the planning committee as well and adjust your schedule accordingly.

Note also that some of the sixteen tasks may be completed at the same time. If you decide to work on more than one task at a time, reflect that on the chart. A Gantt chart lets you see how the tasks relate to each other.

Review the chart carefully when you are finished. Does it look realistic? Is it likely that all of the tasks can be accomplished within the estimated time frame?

If you complete your technology plan at the basic level of effort and within the recommended time frames for each task, the entire planning process should take three to four months. Certainly, your planning process should take no longer than six months. Given the speed with which technology changes, if your process goes on past that point, many of your initial planning assumptions may be inaccurate by the time you finish the process.

What Resources Do You Need to Develop the Plan?

The two primary resources required to develop your plan are money and time, and there is a direct relationship between the two. If you have the money to hire a consultant to manage your planning process, you can allocate less staff and committee time to the project. On the other hand, if you don't have the money to pay for a consultant, the staff and committee will have to do considerably more. You can balance your time and money expenditures depending on your local conditions and resources.

Whatever your decisions, some money will be required. You will need to budget funds for photocopying and printing the final plan. You may also want to provide funding to reimburse nonstaff committee members for their travel mileage or to provide the committee with refreshments. If you have decided to use outside assistance, you will need to budget for that cost as well. If you are planning on using your staff as members of the planning committee or to support the planning committee efforts, you may want to budget for temporary help or overtime costs. If you can't afford to pay for temporary help or overtime costs, you will want to work with the staff who will be involved in the planning process to determine which of their current responsibilities will be reassigned or temporarily discontinued during the planning process. It is neither fair nor realistic to expect staff to add significant planning responsibilities to all of their other assignments without making some adjustments in ongoing responsibilities.

The money for the planning process does not need to come from the library operating budget. You may be able to get a grant from the state library agency or other granting body to help with the planning process. You might also ask the Friends of the Library to help support the planning effort. See Task 14: Develop a Plan for Obtaining the Needed Resources for further information on identifying sources of outside funding for technology activities.

TASK 2
Select the Technology Planning Committee Members

When you complete this task you will have selected a planning committee chairperson. You will also have identified the people who should serve on the planning committee and asked them to serve.

Who is responsible for Task 2?

The library director normally selects the committee, often with the assistance of the planning committee chair.

Who else is involved in Task 2?

Senior staff members may also be involved in deciding which staff should participate on the committee. If you have decided to include community members on the committee, you may want to involve the board in the selection of these people.

What data is needed for Task 2?

You will need an assessment of the skills and knowledge of potential committee members.

What workforms are used in Task 2?

Workform A: Planning Process Worksheet

What outside assistance would be helpful in Task 2?

None

How long will Task 2 take?

The task will take approximately two weeks and will be completed prior to the first meeting of the planning committee.

Is This a Staff Committee, a Community Committee, or Both?

Before you can decide who should serve on the technology planning committee, you need to review again why you are involved in this planning process. As noted in the Introduction, if you intend to follow the process suggested in *Wired for the Future* with little or no modification, you will be developing a plan that will meet the management needs of the library. As a result, this plan will probably require a different type of committee than you would appoint to develop a broad-based library service plan.

There is a big difference between planning for library services and planning to determine what technology is required to provide those services. Library service planning committee members are making decisions about library service priorities and programs intended to meet community needs; thus, the library benefits greatly from broader participation from community and staff. Library technology planning, on the other hand, is primarily a matter of resource management. Therefore, it is likely that many of the members appointed to this technology planning committee will be staff members, although you may also decide to ask others who bring a special expertise or skill to participate in the committee, for example, an individual with a disability who uses adaptive technology.

In some special cases, the library director may decide not to appoint a planning committee at all but rather to give the full responsibility for developing the technology plan to one or two staff members. This would be most likely to occur in a larger library that has one or more full-time positions responsible for managing the library's technological infrastructure. Even so, it will be important for the staff member(s) to involve other library staff members in the planning efforts by appointing special task forces to look at specific parts of the planning process. For example, a task force composed of senior staff could be convened to complete Task 5: Determine Which Activities Require Technology-Based Solutions. A different task force might be formed to complete Task 14: Develop a Plan for Obtaining the Needed Resources. Although the process developed in this book was written with the assumption that it would be used by a planning committee, individuals responsible for developing a library's technology plan will also find the procedure to be a valuable tool. The only adjustments they will need to make will be in the process decisions at the beginning of each planning task.

Who Should Chair the Committee?

The most important committee appointment to be made is the committee chair. The chair needs to be someone who is familiar with technology issues and with library technology applications. He or she also should have good people skills and a track record of successfully managing projects. It is very likely that this will be a staff member, although there may be instances in which a board member would be an effective chair. In small and medium-sized libraries the chair may be the library director. In larger libraries, it will probably be someone other than the director. Once the planning committee chair has been appointed, the library director and the chair (if different people) will work together to make the rest of the committee appointments.

Who Should Serve on the Committee?

Several underlying issues will need to be resolved before you begin to select people to serve on the technology planning committee. The first is the question of technical expertise.

> Do you want all of the committee members to share a similar level of understanding about technology?
>
> If so, how are you going to define that level?
>
> Will you expect the technical expertise to include library-specific applications?

There is no question that it would be very nice to have a technology planning committee made up of people who had a common understanding of library technology issues and who could move quickly to make the decisions required in this planning process. However, it is very unlikely that is going to happen. Instead, you will be selecting your committee members from among the library's public services staff, technical services staff, and technology support staff; each will bring different information and strengths to the process. Even if you are in a small library with three or four people serving all of these staff functions, each person will bring specialized skills and interests. If you expand your committee to include nonstaff members, they too are likely to bring unique talents to the process.

As you review the staff who might be appointed to the committee, consider the following. You will probably want to have representatives from the public services section who have a broad understanding of the library's diverse clientele and the way the current services and programs are being used. If the library is currently using technology to provide some services or programs, the staff involved in using that technology should be represented. You will also want representatives from your technical services section who are familiar with how library technology applications affect access to information and how new technology applications may have an impact on the library's acquisitions and cataloging functions. Finally, if you are fortunate enough to have one or more staff members who are specifically responsible for managing your library's technology infrastructure, you will want to have them represented. If you have enough technical experts so that you have to choose from among them, select those who can communicate most effectively about technology with those who are less familiar with technology issues.

Many public libraries have staff members with specific areas of expertise. The staff from the section serving special populations may know a lot about adaptive technology for the visually or hearing impaired, staff working with children will be very familiar with software for children, and staff working with periodicals will have expertise in that area. The staff responsible for maintaining your current automation system (if you have one) will also have a wealth of specialized information. It is not necessary for all of these people to serve as members of the committee for them to participate in the process. They can be asked to make presentations to the committee or to attend meetings in which their areas of expertise are being discussed.

When considering whether you want to include nonstaff members in the planning process, start by deciding what their role in the process will be. In most cases this will be driven by the skills that your staff representatives bring to the committee. If you are in a small library and have automated few if any of your services or programs, you may need to include one or more nonstaff members with technology expertise on your committee. In that case, you might want to review the list of sources of outside assistance earlier in this chapter. One or more of those people might be effective committee members.

When you have finished juggling all of these criteria, you will probably end up with a technology planning committee that includes members with varying degrees of technical expertise in a number of different areas. The committee members may also have differing understandings of library services and programs. If the technology planning committee does not include members with all of the expertise needed to complete each of the sixteen tasks in this planning process, you will need to decide when it will be appropriate to bring in outside experts and note that on Workform A: Planning Process Worksheet.

Appointments

You are now ready to make your committee appointments. If you are asking staff members to serve on the committee you will use whatever process you normally use to make staff assignments. If, on the other hand, you are asking community members to serve on the committee, you will want to call and discuss the committee appointment with them before sending them an official invitation to serve on the committee. (There is more information on appointing community members to serve on a library committee in chapter 1 of *Planning for Results: A Public Library Transformation Process.*)[1] You might find it helpful to develop a short fact sheet about the process that you can give to people when you ask them to serve on the technology planning committee. The fact sheet could include the purpose of the process, a general time line, the names of the other committee members, and the time and place of the first meeting.

TASK 3
Provide an Orientation for the Planning Committee

When you complete this task you will have evaluated the strengths and weaknesses of your planning committee and designed an orientation process to ensure they have the information they need to develop an effective library plan.

Who is responsible for Task 3?

The library director and the planning chair normally work together to complete this task.

Who else is involved in Task 3?

The members of the planning committee will participate in the orientation.

What data is needed for Task 3?

An assessment of the skills and knowledge of potential committee members is needed.

What workforms are used in Task 3?

Workform A: Planning Process Worksheet

What outside assistance would be helpful in Task 3?

Library staff members with special expertise or outside experts may be asked to participate in the orientation process.

How long will Task 3 take?

The design of the orientation may take up to a week. The preliminary orientation will occur during the first meeting of the committee. Depending on the needs of the committee, additional subject-specific orientation activities may be included in future meetings.

What Do the Committee Members Need to Know?

The committee orientation has two purposes: First, you want to ensure that all of the committee members understand the library technology planning process. Unless one or more of your committee members has used this manual before, you can assume that all of your committee members will need to be introduced to *Wired for the Future.* Second, you want to help all of the committee members develop a common understanding of library technology and current library operations. It may not be easy to determine what constitutes this understanding of library technology and operations.

When you selected the committee members, you looked at their areas of expertise and tried to ensure that the committee as a whole was familiar with all aspects of library technology and with current library operations. Now you need to look at the individual committee members. Are all of the committee members also staff members? If so, any orientation you provide to current library operations will be very different than it will be if the committee includes community members. Regardless of whether all of your committee members are staff members or not, it is very likely that their level of technical expertise will vary widely. What is the base level of information they need to be effective on this committee? Before you can design the orientation for the committee, you have to determine precisely what they need to know.

It will probably be easiest to start by defining the minimum that the committee members will have to know about current library practices. For a staff committee, this might include current statistics on library usage, a copy of the current budget, and a discussion of the current technology-based services and programs. If your committee includes community members, you will want to broaden that to include information on the library's governance, the number of branches the library has, the number and classifications of staff members, and a brief overview of current services and programs.

It will be more difficult to define the minimum level of understanding about library technology the committee members will require. First, to understand library technology, the members of the committee will need to understand something about the technology in general and about technology trends. Second, technology is not a single issue. It breaks into dozens of subsets, each of which can be further subdivided. For example, the subset "network" can be subdivided into local area networks, wide area networks, telecommunications services, and Internet services. (See the Tech Notes near the back of this book.) It is even harder to predict future trends. Stephen Manes, *PC World* contributing editor, says

> The problem with predicting anything more than gross trends
> is the complexity of the real world. Extending current growth
> curves to infinity rarely works—something always comes along
> to change the curves. Pundits often ignore things competitive
> that can turn their predictions to dust. Ultimately, the limiting
> factor for the future isn't hardware or software; it's creativity.[2]

This situation is further complicated by the fact that this is a working committee charged with identifying ways to use technology to accomplish the library's service priorities. By its very nature, the committee will be working within a restricted time frame. The members will not have the luxury of extensive study and review.

What, then, should you do? One solution is to decide that first you want all of the committee members to have a general understanding of how public libraries are using technology-based services and programs to provide a range of services right now. You might then decide that the committee members should also know a little about the technology infrastructures that are required to provide those services and programs. Using this as the foundation, you can then provide more information about specific technology applications and trends at appropriate points in the process.

How Can You Provide the Information the Committee Needs to Know?

To ensure that all of the committee members hear the same thing at the same time, you will want to schedule a formal orientation meeting. The orientation meeting will probably take two to four hours, depending on the makeup of the committee and the amount of basic information they need about the library.

The first step in the orientation is to explain the library technology plan process as developed in *Wired for the Future*. It is imperative that the committee chair have a copy of the manual, and it would be good if other committee members could have one as well.

After you have provided an overview of the process, you will want to distribute copies of the completed Workform A: Planning Process Worksheet. Review the worksheet with the committee, explaining why you made the decisions you did. Encourage the committee to discuss the information on the worksheet and to suggest revisions or changes.

This will provide an excellent opportunity to explain to the members of the committee that in the process outlined in this book, each new task builds on the preceding tasks. The initial tasks are based on assumptions. As the committee proceeds through the process, it will collect increasingly specific data and then will begin to make decisions based on those data. Explain that the process will end by determining what resources are needed to implement the decisions. Inevitably this will mean that new information or discussions during some tasks will require that you revisit earlier tasks. This is a form of continual validation and will help ensure that your recommendations are both consistent and realistic.

The second part of the orientation process will focus on the library. All of the members of the committee should receive a copy of the library service plan during the orientation. Then someone (the director, the chair of the committee that developed the library service plan, or the technology committee chair) should review the major points in the plan. The committee members should have a general understanding of the library goals, objectives, major activities, and resource allocation priorities. Many of the decisions that will be made during this technology planning process will be driven by the service priorities in your library service plan. It is critical that all of the committee members understand those priorities. If you don't have a recent library services plan, read the section What Should You Do if You Haven't Selected Service Priorities and Identified Activities? in chapter 2.

The third part of the orientation will address technology issues. Start by asking each member of the committee to briefly discuss his or her area of technology expertise. Then ask someone who is well-versed in technology *and* able to discuss technology issues in easily assessable terms to lead a general discussion of the current state of library technology and of general technology trends. It would be very helpful if you could send the committee members one or more articles on these issues before the orientation meeting. You may find such articles by checking some of the resources suggested in Task 7: Become Familiar with Current Technologies and Developing Trends. You might also develop a one- or two-page handout that defines the various infrastructure options available to the library (Internet, CD-ROM, etc.) and include it in the mailing to the committee.

It is clear that the members of this committee will need to develop and maintain a broad understanding of the technologies that affect libraries to complete this process and that this general introduction only scratches the surface of what they will need to know. Does that mean that you have to postpone the process for six months or a year while the members learn everything they can? Certainly not. The planning process in which you are all involved will be a significant learning experience. As you explore the options open to the library and discuss the ramifications of those options, you will be developing the foundation for the broad understanding of the technology you need to make decisions.

Before adjourning the orientation meeting, encourage the committee members to begin to study on their own. You might want to give the members a copy of the Bibliography for this manual. Finally, ask the committee members to identify areas in which they need more information as they go through this process, then schedule short mini-orientation programs to provide the requested information, as needed.

NOTES

1. Ethel Himmel and William James Wilson, *Planning for Results: A Public Library Transformation Process* (Chicago: ALA, 1998).

2. Stephen Manes, "The Future of PCs? Don't Ask Me," *PC World* 16 (Jan. 1998): 372.

Chapter 2

Identifying Technology Needs

MILESTONES

By the time you complete this chapter you should

- understand the relationship between your library service priorities and your technology plan

- understand the general framework of *Planning for Results: A Public Library Transformation Process*

- know how to determine which of your activities might be implemented using technology

- understand why you need to know where you are now before you begin to plan and learn how to determine your current conditions

Every Library Is Unique

Every public library serves a different community, and each community is unique. Each library has identified different goals, objectives, and activities, just as each has staff with different skills and has collections with different areas of emphasis. The financial resources that libraries have also vary widely, as do their current levels of technology. Because of these differences, there can be no such thing as a one-size-fits-all planning process for technology—or for any other library function. Each library must start this process from where it is now and base its decisions on the outcomes it wants in the future.

As a basis for your planning, you need to have a clear and comprehensive picture of the current status of technology in your own library. You also need to understand your library's service priorities and the outcomes you are working toward. Remember, once again: technology is not an end in itself. It is a tool (and only one of several tools, at that) to support the activities that you have determined will meet the unique needs of your community.

The issue that will be addressed in the second planning step is that of Identifying Technology Needs. The three tasks you need to complete to accomplish this step are

TASK 4
Review the Library Service Goals, Objectives, and Activities

TASK 5
Determine Which Activities Require Technology-Based Solutions

TASK 6
Assess Your Current Conditions

TASK 4
Review the Library Service Goals, Objectives, and Activities

During this task you will become familiar with the library service priorities, the activities planned to support those priorities, and the measures the library will use to measure the success of the activities.

Who will be responsible for Task 4?
The planning committee chairperson will lead this task.

Who else will be involved in Task 4?

The members of the planning committee will be involved. The library director and staff members will be involved in prioritizing the library activities.

> *Enhanced level of effort:* If you do not have a library service plan, you will want to involve the library administration and members of the public service staff in the process of selecting service responses and identifying activities; another committee or a subcommittee of the planning committee may be appointed to manage that process.

What data is required for Task 4?

The library service plan provides the data.

> *Enhanced level of effort:* If you do not have a library service plan, you will need to select service responses and identify activities.

What workforms are used in Task 4?

None

What outside assistance would be helpful in Task 4?

It might be helpful to have the chair or another representative from the committee that developed the library service plan join the technology committee as it determines the library's technology needs. Such a representative could provide useful insight into the discussions that led to the recommendations in the service plan.

> *Enhanced level of effort:* If you have to select service responses and identify activities, you may want to hire a planning consultant to assist with this part of the process.

How long will Task 4 take?

This task can be accomplished in one meeting if the members of the committee receive the service plan prior to the meeting.

> *Enhanced level of effort:* If you do not have a library service plan, you cannot complete this task until you have selected service responses and identified activities. That will probably take an additional two to four weeks.

What Do the Library Service Priorities Have to Do with the Technology Plan?

As stated elsewhere, the underlying assumption in this technology planning process is that technology is not an end in itself. Rather, technology is a tool that will help you provide services and programs to meet your community's needs. If you think about it, this makes a lot of sense. There are literally hundreds of technology products and services available to the library, and there are a variety of technology infrastructures you might establish to provide those services and products. If you don't have a clear understanding of what you are trying to accomplish, it will be difficult to know what criteria to apply when trying to select from among all of your choices.

Therefore, before you can begin to plan you need to know what your library is trying to accomplish and how those accomplishments will be measured. This will be easy if your library has recently completed a general planning process. The assumption throughout this manual is that you have used *Planning for Results: A Public Library Transformation Process* as the framework for your planning process.[1] However, it is not a requirement for completing this technology planning process. You may use any current service plan that you have for your library to identify your technology needs. Some libraries are still using *Planning and Role-Setting for Public Libraries* (McClure and others) to guide their planning efforts.[2] Other libraries have used strategic planning models provided by their city or county governments. Yet other libraries have hired organization-development consultants to manage their planning activities. Some libraries have not completed a full formal planning process but have developed a list of goals, objectives, and activities. The general planning process used is not important; what *is* important in terms of determining your technology needs is the fact that you have selected service priorities and identified an array of activities that support those priorities.

What Should You Do if You Haven't Selected Service Priorities and Identified Activities?

If your library has not completed a library service plan recently, do you have to stop your technology planning until you develop such a plan? Absolutely not! You will, however, have to complete Task 4 at an enhanced level of effort to select service priorities and identify activities that support those priorities before you continue. A description of that enhanced level of effort follows.

How Can You Determine Your Service Priorities?

The most effective way for your library to determine its service priorities is to base your discussion on the thirteen public library service responses that were introduced in *Planning for Results: A Public Library Transformation Process.*[3] Service responses are defined as

> what a library does for, or offers to, the public in an effort to meet a set of well-defined community needs. . . . They represent the gathering and deployment of specific critical resources to produce a specific public benefit or result.[4]

The thirteen service responses in *Planning for Results* are

Basic Literacy   A library that offers Basic Literacy service addresses the need to read and to perform other essential daily tasks.

Business and Career Information   A library that offers Business and Career Information service addresses a need for information related to business, careers, work, entrepreneurship, personal finances, and obtaining employment.

Commons   A library that provides a Commons environment helps address the need of people to meet and interact with others in their community and to participate in public discourse about community issues.

Community Referral   A library that offers Community Referral addresses the need for information related to services provided by community agencies and organizations.

Consumer Information   A library that provides Consumer Information service helps to satisfy the need for information that affects the ability of community residents to make informed consumer decisions and to help them become more self-sufficient.

Cultural Awareness   A library that offers Cultural Awareness service helps satisfy the desire of community residents to gain an understanding of their own cultural heritage and the cultural heritage of others.

Current Topics and Titles   A library that provides Current Topics and Titles helps to fulfill community residents' appetite for information about popular cultural and social trends and their desire for satisfying recreational experiences.

Formal Learning Support   A library that offers Formal Learning Support helps students who are enrolled in a formal program of education or who are pursuing their education through a program of home schooling to attain their educational goals.

General Information   A library that offers General Information helps meet the need for information and answers to questions on a broad array of topics related to work, school, and personal life.

Government Information   The library that offers Government Information service helps satisfy the need for information about elected officials and governmental agencies that enable people to participate in the democratic process.

Information Literacy A library that provides Information Literacy service helps address the need for skills related to finding, evaluating, and using information effectively.

Lifelong Learning A library that provides Lifelong Learning service helps address the desire for self-directed personal growth and development opportunities.

Local History and Genealogy A library that offers Local History and Genealogy service addresses the desire of community residents to know and better understand personal or community heritage.

In addition to these thirteen service responses, *Planning for Results* provides a process to help libraries develop personalized service responses to describe unique services or programs. It also provides extensive information about each of these service responses including the following:

- example of the need addressed
- what the library does and provides
- some possible components
- target audiences and service aspects
- resource allocation issues to consider, further subdivided by staff, collection/information resources, facilities, and technology
- possible measures to consider
- stories describing how actual libraries provide the service

Who Will Be Involved in the Selection of Service Responses?

The selection of service responses is not the responsibility of the technology planning committee, although one or more of the committee members may be involved. If service responses must be selected, representatives from the library board, library administration, and the various public service sections of the library should be involved in the selection. The library director will appoint someone to lead that process and will decide who else to involve in the selection process.

How Will the Service Responses Be Selected?

The person managing the process to select service responses will want to read *Planning for Results* carefully, paying special attention to the sections that address the service responses. For this very abbreviated process, the service responses can probably be selected in a single meeting. Because service responses are intended to meet specific community needs, it would be helpful to prepare a brief (one- or two-page) profile of the community. The participants should receive a copy of the community profile and a summary of the service responses prior to the meeting.

The meeting will begin with a review of the community profile and a discussion of community needs. The group will then discuss each of the service responses. Finally, the group will select the three to five service responses that most effectively address the identified community needs. Several suggested processes to help groups reach agreement on service responses are included in the How-To section of *Planning for Results.*

Who Will Identify the Activities for Each Service Response?

The person responsible for identifying service response activities will depend on the size of your library. In a large library with multiple units, the director may ask a different group of staff members to draft a list of activities for each service response. For example, if the library has selected Business and Career Information as a service response, the director might ask several people from the business section and two or three adult services librarians from the branches to work together to identify possible activities. On the other hand, in a smaller library, the same group that selected the service responses might be asked to identify activities. Once this group (or groups) has developed a preliminary list, the activities should be reviewed and refined by the library director and senior staff members.

Do You Have to Develop Objectives?

In *Planning for Results,* objectives indicate how the library will measure its progress toward reaching a goal. In *Wired for the Future,* this measure is important because it indicates the desired outcomes from the activity. For example, the activity "provide homework help for students" might be measured by the total number of students receiving such help or by the number of individual students receiving such help. It could also be measured by the impact of the help: Did the student find what he or she needed? In a timely manner? Finally, it could be measured by the use of the library's resources: the number of hits on the library homework Web page or the circulation figures for special curriculum-support collections. The implementation of the activity will vary depending on the measure.

The library does not have to develop formal objectives, but it would be very helpful if the group that refines the list of activities also indicates the most important measures of success for each. When they have finished with that, you will be ready to continue with the *Wired for the Future* process. You will use your list of service responses, activities, and measures of success in place of the library service plan during the remainder of this task and Task 5: Determine Which Activities Require Technology-Based Solutions.

What Are You Looking for When You Review the Goals, Objectives, and Activities?

It is probable that the library's service plan (or service responses and activities) was developed by a completely different group of people from your current committee. Therefore, the first thing to do is to ask each of the members of the technology planning committee to read the service plan carefully. Remind the committee members that the technology choices you will be making will be driven by the outcomes identified in the service plan.

As you read the service plan, pay special attention to the goals, objectives, and activities. If your plan was based on *Planning for Results,* the goals will describe the outcome your community will receive because the library provides a specific service response. The objectives indicate how the library will measure its progress toward reaching a goal. The activities are the strategies or actions that the library will carry out to achieve its objectives. For example, let's assume that your library has selected Business and Career Information as a service response. Libraries that select this service response address the need for information related to business, careers, work, entrepreneurship, personal finances, and obtaining employment. Your library might have chosen to target its services specifically to the business community by developing a goal that stated: "Business owners in Anytown will have the information they need to run their businesses in an efficient and effective manner." The objectives for this goal might include

At least 20 percent of the small-business owners in Anytown will indicate on a survey that they used the library for business-related information during the past year.

At least 75 percent of the small-business owners in Anytown who reported that they used the library to find business-related information in the past year will say that information was available to them in a convenient location.

The number of business reference questions answered will increase from *XX* to *XX* during this fiscal year.

There could be anywhere from two to a dozen activities in the plan under this goal and these objectives. These activities will serve as the basis for the committee's technology needs assessment process.

TASK 5
Determine Which Activities Require Technology-Based Solutions

In this task, the committee will identify and prioritize the activities that will use technology-based solutions to make progress toward reaching the library's goals.

Who will be responsible for Task 5?

The technology planning committee chairperson will take the lead in this task.

Who else will be involved in Task 5?

The members of the technology planning committee will participate. It will also be helpful to include senior staff members from the areas that are, or will be, involved in implementing these activities to join in the discussion. When the draft list of activities has been completed, it will be presented to the library director for approval.

What data is needed for Task 5?

The library service plan will supply the data.

What workforms are used in Task 5?

Workform C: Library Technology Needs
Workform D: Library Technology Needs Summary
Workform E: Forced Choices Process

What outside assistance would be helpful in Task 5?

This is a task in which an outside facilitator might be helpful. The committee will be involved in extensive review and discussion with the intent of reaching consensus.

How long will Task 5 take?

This task can be completed in the same meeting as Task 4.

What Should You Consider
When Reviewing Activities?

As noted earlier, the technology planning committee is not responsible for determining the needs of the community or the service priorities to meet those needs. That work has (or should have been) done by others. The technology planning committee is specifically responsible for ensuring that the library uses technology effectively and efficiently to reach the library's desired outcomes. Because of this scope, the technology committee's recommendations will flow from the activities in the broader plan.

Before you begin this review process, you need to determine who will be involved. Senior members of the public services and technical services staff will be helpful in this review process. These are the people who are ultimately responsible for implementing the activities, and their perspective will be valuable, both in reviewing proposed activities and in determining the priority of the activities being considered.

Start the review process by completing a separate copy of Workform C: Library Technology Needs for each goal and the objectives that will measure the progress toward reaching that goal. List the activities in your library service plan that are intended to accomplish that goal in the space provided on the workform. You will want to list only activities that have not yet been implemented.

In many cases, library service plans only include services to be provided to the public; these plans may not include activities relating to purchasing or upgrading an automated circulation system, providing an online public access catalog, automating the acquisitions process, or streamlining cataloging and processing activities. Yet, you will certainly want to address these management activities as you develop your technology plan. If your library service plan focuses on services to the public, use a separate copy of Workform C to record these management activities with technology components. In the space provided for the goal, write "Management technology." You can leave the objectives blank, but be sure to list the activities in the spaces provided.

Make copies of all the completed workforms and distribute them to the members of the committee and the others you have invited to participate in this process. Ask each participant to look again at the goal (desired outcome) and the objectives (measures of progress toward reaching the outcome). Are there other activities that might be effective in reaching the desired outcomes? It is possible that the members of the technology planning committee, because of their special expertise, will be able to identify additional activities that could help the library reach its goals. It may simply be that there are products or services available now that were not available when the service plan was being developed. In this rapidly changing environment, the activities a library undertakes to accomplish its desired outcomes must remain flexible. If you do identify additional activities, note them in the spaces provided on Workform C. Finally, indicate which activities will "definitely" *require* technology to implement and which *could* be implemented using technology.

You will probably want to spend a part of one of your meetings discussing each of the committee member's responses to Workform C. As you review each of the goals, objectives, and activities, keep a record of the committee's decisions as to which activities will require technology-based solutions, which activities should be revised and what those revisions were, and what new activities were identified. When you are through, you should have a composite Workform C for each goal, reflecting the committee consensus.

What Do You Do if the Activities in Your Service Plan Are Too Specific?

As you review the activities you have listed on Workform C, you may find that some of them already presuppose a specific technology solution. For example, an activity under the Business and Career Information service goal and objectives might be

Make full-text business periodicals available on CD-ROM.

Does such an activity mean that the decision has already been made for the technology committee and that you don't need to review it further? Not necessarily. The library service plan was developed by a different group of people with different areas of expertise from those of the members of the library technology committee. Furthermore, the library service plan could have been developed as long as two or three years ago, which is a very long time in terms of technology options. As noted previously, the technology planning committee is responsible for recommending the best technology options to accomplish the library's outcomes right now, and there are a variety of ways of accomplishing most activities. You don't have to enumerate the other options now. (You will be doing that in Task 7: Become Familiar with Current Technologies and Developing Trends.) What you do need to do now is revise the *activity* to leave the technology solution open. In the example above, you might revise the activity to read

Make full-text business periodicals available.

What if None of the Activities Appear to Require Technology-Based Solutions?

It is unlikely, but not impossible, that the library service plan would not include at least some activities requiring technology. It is even more unlikely that the board or director of a library that had such a plan would decide to develop a library technology plan. However, if you find yourself in this situation, the first thing to do is look at the date the library service plan was developed. If it is more than eighteen months old, it may not provide the direction needed to make technology decisions, and you will have to complete the enhanced level of effort in Task 4: Review the Library Service Goals, Objectives, and Activities.

If the plan was completed recently, look carefully at the goals and objectives. Remember that the technology committee can identify new activities that will help the library reach its desired outcomes. When considering additional activities, it might be helpful to review the appropriate sections of *Planning for Results*.

Are All of the Activities Equally Important?

You probably finished your review of Workform C with a list of at least fifteen or twenty activities that require technology-based solutions. The next step in the process is to merge all of these activities into a single prioritized list on Workform D: Library Technology Needs Summary.

You can determine the priority of the activities in a number of ways. You might want to start by looking again at the library service plan. If the goals are listed in priority order, it is possible that at least some of the activities that support Goal 1 are more important than the activities that support Goals 2 or 3. Next look at the activities themselves. By the very nature of activities, some are fairly significant and some are less important. Judge their relative value by deciding which activities will have the most impact on meeting the outcomes (goals) identified in the library service plan.

If the committee members are having trouble deciding which activities are most important, you might want to ask them each to complete Workform E: Forced Choices Process. This optional process allows the committee members to rate each activity against every other activity, resulting in a priority ranking. When the committee members have completed Workform E, ask them to discuss their rankings and reach agreement on which activities are likely to have the most impact. If they still cannot reach consensus, average the individual rankings for each committee member to determine an average ranking for each activity.

When the committee has completed ranking the activities through whatever process worked for them, list the activities in priority order in the first column of Workform D. This listing will be used as the basis for Task 7: Become Familiar with Current Technologies and Developing Trends.

The second column on Workform D is headed "Measure(s) of Success." In this column, you will note how the library intends to measure the success of each of the activities requiring technology-based solutions. These measures will be found in the objectives of your service plan.

To continue with the earlier example, the three objectives under the Business and Career Information services goal were

At least 20 percent of the small-business owners in Anytown will indicate on a survey that they used the library for business-related information during the past year.

At least 75 percent of the small-business owners in Anytown who reported that they used the library to find business-related information in the past year will say that information was available to them in a convenient location.

The number of business reference questions answered will increase from XX to XX during this fiscal year.

In the first objective, the measure is "total number of users"; in the second, the measure is "convenient access"; and in the third, the measure is "reference questions answered."

Now look again at the activities and match the measures in the objectives to the activities. For instance, the activity "Provide access to full-text business journals" would probably be measured by both the total number of users and by its convenient access. As you identify one or more measures of success, write them in the appropriate box on Workform D. (You will use this form again in Task 8: Evaluate the Options for Your Highest Priority Activities.)

Who Should Review and Approve Workform D?

Because the information on Workform D will form the foundation for the rest of this planning process, it is important that it accurately reflects the priorities of the library director or library board. The committee chair should present the final draft of Workform D to the library director for review and approval. The director may want to meet with the committee to discuss the process used to reach consensus on the priorities reflected on the workform. When Workform D has been approved, consider distributing it to all staff members with a short explanation of how it will be used to continue the process.

TASK 6
Assess Your Current Conditions

In this task you will inventory your current hardware, software, and networks; assess the technology skills of your staff and the public you serve; and evaluate how ready your facility(ies) is to accommodate technology.

You will conclude this task with an exercise that will help you put all of this information into a planning context.

Who is responsible for Task 6?

The planning committee chair and/or the library director will be responsible for assigning staff to complete Workforms F and G. The planning committee chair will be responsible for leading the Facility SWOT analysis (Workform H) (strengths, weaknesses, opportunities, and threats) portion of this task.

Who else is involved in Task 6?

The committee members will review all data collected in the Workforms to become familiar with the current level of technology in the library.

What data is needed for Task 6?

Needed data include information about the current hardware, software, and networks in each of the library's facilities. Also needed is information about the library facilities and about the technology skills of the staff and the public.

What workforms are used in Task 6?

Workform F: Current Technology Overview
Workform G: Facility Review
Workform H: SWOT Analysis of the Library Technology Environment

What outside assistance would be helpful in Task 6?

Library technology staff members may be assigned to complete Workforms F and G. You may also need to involve electricians, air-conditioning experts, etc., in the review. The library director and other staff members may be included in the SWOT (strengths, weaknesses, opportunities, and threats) analysis to complete Workform H.

How long will Task 6 take?

The workforms should be completed in a week or two. A part of one committee meeting will focus on reviewing the information on the workforms.

Why Do You Need to Know What You Have?

Every new technology-based product or service you consider will have a set of requirements that must be met before you can use it. These requirements might include one or more of the following: hardware, software, a network, telephone connections, or changes to your building(s). Technologies will often require certain staff skills to install or operate them. Before you choose new technology products to support your services, it is important to ensure that you have the prerequisites in place to use the products. Assessing your readiness to adopt a new product or service begins by creating an inventory of the hardware, software, network(s), building wiring, and telephone connections you already have. These elements are also sometimes known as the library's "technology infrastructure."

It is also important that you inventory your staff's technical skills. Many products assume a familiarity with certain standard computer techniques, such as how to use a mouse or the basics of a Windows interface, including drop-down menus and selection buttons. You will want to know which skills and experience each member of your staff has. You will also need to estimate the computer skills of your public. The most-advanced product choices won't serve the community's needs if the public doesn't know how to use them. If you choose products that will require teaching the public, it is important that you allocate time and resources to provide that training.

Completing an accurate assessment of your current technology infrastructure, of the current staff technology skills, and of the readiness of your building to accommodate new technology are the essential first steps in this process. In Task 10: Determine What It Will Cost to Implement the Proposed Infrastructure, you will need to refer back to this inventory. It will assist you in determining what, if any, additional equipment and software you will need to establish your proposed technology infrastructure.

You will use Workform F: Current Technology Overview to record the information about the library's technology infrastructure and about staff and user skills. You will use Workform G: Facility Review to record information about your current facility(ies); complete a separate copy of Workform G for each facility in your library system. You will only complete one copy for the central or main library even if the facility has several floors or a number of relatively autonomous departments. As noted at the beginning of this task, multiple staff or committee members may be involved in gathering this data and completing these forms. When the forms have been completed, each committee member should receive copies of all the forms.

What Do You Have Now?

Completing Workform F: Current Technology Overview

Most libraries have some type of computer hardware installed now, if only a single personal computer used for word processing. In developing a current technology overview, it is important to include all of the equipment you have that is working, even if that equipment is presently being used only for office automation applications. As your technology plan develops, you may find a good use for an older machine, allowing you to recycle equipment to new uses.

Libraries with automated systems often have both end-user equipment on desktops and one or more additional computers dedicated to managing the library's database, CD-ROMs, or Web pages. To distinguish between these devices, the desktop machines are often referred to as "client" devices, while the computers managing the resources are called "servers." This distinction is made in Workform F to help you gather and record data. A fuller discussion of client/server computing can be found in the Tech Notes.

Part 1: Client Devices and Software

Use Part 1 of Workform F to identify each client (end-user) device you have in each facility in the library. Part 1 is divided into two sections: Client Devices and Client Software. You will need to complete a copy of Part 1 for *each* device in a facility. If you have more than one facility, note on the facility line the facility in which the device is housed. Use the location line to indicate where the machine is located (circulation desk, reference desk, etc.).

Record the manufacturer and model number, if you have it, of each device in the Description box.

Client Devices

Character-Based Terminal

A character-based terminal (dumb terminal) is a device that end users use to communicate with a computer, typically a minicomputer or mainframe. The terminal accepts keyboard input from the user and sends it to a computer. The computer processes the keystrokes and returns output to be displayed on the terminal's screen. The character-based terminal has no processing capacity of its own and must be used in conjunction with a computer.

The description of a terminal might be Wyse 30 or IBM 3476.

PROTOCOL

The "rules" governing the exchange of keystrokes and the display of information on character-based terminals are called "protocols." The most common terminal protocols in library applications are VT100 and VT420.

Personal Computer (PC)

A personal computer has processing capacity and can stand alone. The description of a PC might be Compaq 486, IBM PS/2, or Power Macintosh 7500.

PROCESSOR TYPE AND SPEED

Processor type refers to the kind of computer chip in the machine. Although not all PC chips are produced by Intel, most are; even those from other suppliers are usually identified as being similar to a specific Intel chip. Intel chips range from model number 8088 (so old it is now in the Smithsonian), through to the current model, which is presently a Pentium II. The common Intel chips in libraries include 286, 386, 486, and Pentium.

Processor speed is a measure of how fast a chip can execute instructions. Processor speeds are expressed in megahertz (MHz). A Pentium chip described as a 180 MHz chip can process software instructions twice as fast as a Pentium 90 MHz chip. As software becomes more complex, the speed with which a chip can execute the instructions becomes crucial. This is especially true with multimedia applications that include sound and video clips, such as a CD-ROM encyclopedia or the Library of Congress American Memory Web site.

RANDOM ACCESS MEMORY (RAM)

RAM is where computers store data being used by the processor. Think of disk storage as a computer's filing cabinet and RAM as the computer's desktop, where it keeps the projects it is actively working on. Accessing data from memory is much faster than accessing data from a disk drive, so software programs are written to bring into memory the instructions or data most likely to be requested next by the processor. The amount of memory available to the processor affects the performance of a program. If the program has to retrieve data from a disk drive because there wasn't enough memory to anticipate the next request, the computer waits while the data is transferred. Most software programs identify the minimum amount of memory they need to operate. Any amount of memory less than the minimum will adversely affect the performance of the program. More memory than the minimum will generally improve a program's performance.

DISK SPACE AVAILABLE

Disk storage is where the programs and data are stored when the computer is not using them. Storage can be fixed or removable. Early computers had only removable storage. With these drives, you could remove the programs and data by taking out the storage medium, a "floppy" disk. Floppy disks were portable; you could take a set of programs or data from one PC to another by simply putting the disks into the second PC's disk drive. Today, a PC's primary storage disk is typically a fixed disk drive, also called a "hard drive." With a hard disk drive, the storage medium is sealed into the drive; the only way to remove data or programs is to copy them to a floppy disk or tape or to delete them entirely.

You need to know how much space you have available to store new programs. Record the storage space available in megabytes on Workform F.

Operating System

The operating system is a set of basic computer instructions that knit together all the pieces of hardware into a functioning computer. Programmers of software applications incorporate the features of the operating system into their programs. This means that applications are written for particular operating systems and will operate only on a computer running that operating system.

Programs written for Apple's Mac OS operating system will not run on a machine that has Microsoft's Windows operating system. Some programs written for Windows 95 will not operate on Windows 3.1. Most programs are written to run under multiple operating systems, but it is important to ensure that the version of any program you select will run on the operating system you have on your server and client workstations.

Color Monitor Resolution

Color monitors are distinguished by their resolution, the number of picture elements (pixels) they can display. VGA monitors can display 640 × 480 (horizontal × vertical) pixels. SVGA monitors can display 800 × 600. Many graphics products require at least SVGA monitors to operate properly.

Sound Card

Many PCs include components that enable the PC to play music or reproduce voices or other sounds. These components are called "sound cards." Most sound cards are capable of reproducing "16-bit" sound, although early cards were capable of only "8-bit" sound. If you have a sound card in a client device, be sure to note it and, if possible, distinguish between 8- and 16-bit cards.

Speakers or Headphones

If a PC has a sound card, note whether speakers *or* headphones are used to broadcast the sound.

Client Software

In addition to the operating system information you noted under Client Device, you should also inventory the software applications you are running on each client PC. These software applications can be divided into three types: IP services, application-specific client software, and general commercial applications.

Use the Description portion of each line to note the version number of the software you are listing and indicate what the software is used for, i.e., Internet access, CD-ROM access, and staff scheduling.

Internet Protocol (IP) Services

IP services are specialized applications used by computers to communicate over networks. The two most common IP services on library client machines are Telnet and HTTP, also known as a Web browser.

TELNET

If your PC is being used as a terminal on a network or over the Internet, you may be running a special service called Telnet, software that permits a PC to emulate a terminal while communicating with another computer over a network. If so, note in the Description which Telnet client you are using. For example, Windows 95 has a Telnet client, WRQ Inc.'s Reflections includes a Telnet client, Rasmussen Software Inc.'s Anzio Lite is a Telnet client. Which Telnet client you are using may be important: different Telnet clients have different features, and some software applications require specific Telnet clients to operate.

BROWSER

If your PC includes a Web browser, note which one it is in the Description line: Netscape's Navigator or Communicator, Microsoft's Internet Explorer, or another browser.

Helper Applications Helper applications extend the functionality of Web browsers. They include Adobe Acrobat, Real Audio, Real Video, etc., and can be launched by the browser as needed to deal with specific formats of files retrieved from the Internet. List applications such as these in the spaces provided. More information on IP applications can be found in the Communications Protocols and TCP/IP Services Tech Note.

Application-Specific Client Software

Application-specific client software includes any proprietary software you may have to operate a product such as your library automation system from a PC. If you are using a vendor's automated system or are accessing CD-ROMs from a PC, you may have loaded special client applications on the PC to access these products. Examples of application client software include CARL's Everybody's Catalog, SeaChange's BookWhere? Z39.50 client, or The Library Corporation's ITS Workstation. CD-ROMs such as Microsoft's Encarta or Delorme's Phone Search USA also install application-specific software on a PC to enable the PC to access data from the CD.

Commercial Applications

Do you have any security software such as Fortres 101, IKIOSK, or a virus detector? What other applications do you have (word processing, spreadsheet, database, access adaptations for people with disabilities, etc.)? List the applications loaded on each machine.

Part 2: Servers and Printers

Identify the servers and printers you have in each facility in the library on Part 2 of Workform F. If you have more than one facility, note the facility in which the server or printer is housed on the facility line.

Servers

The data you need to gather about your server(s) is very similar to the PC requirements described in Part 1.

CD Server

If you have a CD server, you also have to consider the following elements.

NUMBER OF DRIVES

The number of drives determines how many CDs will operate simultaneously.

SPEED

Speed is the rate at which data is transferred off the CD. It is generally referred to by a number followed by *X,* for example, 2X, 12X, 24X. The larger the number, the faster the speed. CDs with a multimedia content require faster transfer rates than CDs that contain only text.

Printers

The information requested about your printers can be found in the documentation that came with them. If you can no longer find that documentation, you will probably be able to find what you need on the manufacturer's Web page. You can also call the manufacturer and request this information from a customer service representative.

Serial or Parallel

The type of direct cable connection between a printer and a workstation may be through serial or parallel ports. Macintosh computers always connect to printers through serial connections; Intel-based computers can use either connection, although parallel connections are more common.

Networked

Sometimes printers can be used by workstations even if there is no cable directly connecting the printer to the workstation. This is possible when multiple workstations on a network can access a printer directly connected to one of the workstations. Printers may also be attached to a network device called a "print server." A print server will allow multiple workstations to print from a single printer. Note on the Workform if any of your printers are networked.

Color

As information resources include more graphic content, color becomes increasingly important in printed documents. Note if any of your printers supports color printing.

Resolution

A printer's resolution is described in the number of dots per inch (dpi) that the printer can put on a page. A typical workstation printer supports 300 dpi on a vertical line and 300 dpi on a horizontal line. This is referred to as a 300 × 300 printer. Printers supporting 600 × 600 provide finer and more-detailed graphic output. Photo-quality printing can be achieved with printers offering resolutions of 1440 × 720. Note the resolution of the printers you have available.

Part 3: Networks

In Part 3 you will inventory your networks, both Local Area Networks (LANs) and Wide Area Networks (WANs). See the Tech Notes for more information about networks. You will need to complete a copy of Workform F Part 3 for each facility that has a LAN.

Every network consists of hardware, software, and cabling to link the components of the network together. WANs add communications elements such as phone lines, cable, or wireless connections to the other components.

Local Area Networks (LANs)

Some libraries have installed LANs to support multiuser access to shared resources such as networked CD-ROMs or to support management functions such as budgeting and word processing. Sometimes libraries have several LANs, each supporting different services or different departments within the library. Occasionally, libraries have LANs without even realizing it. This happens when the library's automation vendor has installed network equipment such as a terminal server to connect character-based terminals, also called "dumb" terminals, to the library's local automated system. It might also happen in branches that have PCs and network communications equipment, like a router, linked together with data cabling to communicate with a remote site. Even if there is no "server" in the branch, it still has a LAN.

All three of the components—hardware, software, and data cabling—need to be included in your inventory of each of your existing LANs. You will use Part 3 of Workform F to gather and record the hardware and software data on any local area networks you may have installed. Workform G: Facility Review will assist you in gathering data about your cabling.

Hubs

The hardware devices in a LAN communicate with each other over data cabling, which can be copper wires, fiber optic cables, or a combination of the two. Although in early networks the data cabling was strung from one device to the next to establish the connection, today it is more common for each device to be cabled to a single piece of equipment, called a "hub," which connects the devices to each other. Hubs can connect four to twenty-four or more devices; large networks often include multiple hubs. Note the number of hubs you have and the number of connections or ports those hubs can support. You may also want to determine how many of those ports are presently unused. The description of the ports might include information on the type of data cable connection the port supports, such as RJ-45 or fiber.

NETWORK TYPE

The type of network is defined by two standards, a Media Access Control (MAC) standard and a data communications standard, also called a "protocol." The MAC standard determines the format of the messages and ensures that only one device at a time tries to pass data so that multiple messages don't collide. The two most common MAC standards are Ethernet and Token Ring. Most libraries use Ethernet; Token Ring is used in IBM networks.

SPEED

Speed is the rate at which data can travel over a network. The common speeds for Ethernet networks are 10 million bits per second (Mbps) and 100 Mbps.

Terminal Servers

Terminal servers are used to connect character-based terminals to a computer over a network. Like hubs, they include a number of ports, typically ranging from eight to sixteen. Your description of these ports should include the type of data cable connection supported, RJ-45 or serial. You may find multiple types of ports on a single terminal server. For example, you may find eight serial ports to support connections to terminals and one RJ-45 port to connect the terminal server to your network.

NETWORK TYPE

Terminal servers are designed to run either the Ethernet protocol or IBM's Token Ring protocol. Ethernet is the most common network protocol in libraries.

SPEED

Terminal servers operate at network speeds. The common speeds for Ethernet networks are 10 Mbps and 100 Mbps.

Network Operating System

In addition to the communication protocols, networked devices need operating-system software that manages the sharing of files or networked devices such as printers. With some PC operating systems, such as Windows for Workgroups, Windows 95 (and later releases of the Microsoft operating system), or

Apple's Mac OS, the networking software is built into the operating system. Networks based on PC operating systems are peer-to-peer networks in which each PC uses its built-in networking features to share its resources with other PCs on its LAN. Other peer-to-peer network software includes LANtastic and NetWare Lite.

Networks in which the shared resources are concentrated in one computer or a few computers but are available to many users may employ specialized network operating system software, such as Novell NetWare or Windows NT. This software manages client/server networks in which applications running on desktop machines (clients) request database access, shared files, or services such as printing, from one or more servers. See the Client Server Computing Tech Notes for more information. Networks in which the server is running the UNIX operating system and the user workstations are using the TCP/IP protocol to communicate with the server are very common in libraries with commercial library automation systems.

Wide Area Networks (WANs)

Libraries often need to connect hardware devices at one site with computers at another site. For example, a multibranch library needs to connect terminals and personal computers in each branch with the library's local system server that is located at a single site. Even single-building libraries may need to connect devices to a remote site such as the Internet or a shared automation system. The communication system that connects devices to each other over distances is called a wide area network (WAN). The links between the sites are most often telephone lines, although the connections can also be established with microwave, radio transmissions, or other wireless communication options.

Internal or External

WANs can be internal networks used to connect multiple libraries to a single site. This type of WAN is common in libraries with multiple branches sharing an automated system or in a consortium of libraries sharing an automated system. WANs can also be used to connect to external resources such as the Internet. Often a library or a consortium of libraries will have both an internal WAN among the facilities and an external WAN connection to the Internet.

MULTIPLEXERS

Some libraries have developed multisite communications networks based on transmitting character-oriented data between sites using multiplexers and telephone lines. Multiplexers provide a way of merging the data from several devices into a single stream that can be transmitted over a phone line. While this works well for the transmissions of text in most library automation systems, it is not a technology that can transmit graphics or sound, including the graphics of the Internet. It is important, therefore, to determine whether existing wide area connections are multiplexing character data or transferring network packet data across the phone lines.

ROUTERS/BRIDGES

A bridge is a device that provides a communication pathway between segments of a network. A bridge can be either local, connecting two or more segments of a LAN in a building, or remote, connecting segments of a network in different locations over telephone lines. Some library automation systems installed in the early 1990s were configured by the vendor with bridging technology connecting branches to the central site. A bridge cannot be used as the connection to the Internet.

Routers also connect segments of a network, but a router provides filtering and traffic-control features not available in bridges. Although bridges still have a place in network design, routers are more commonly used in library networks to connect remote sites. Routers are also used to connect a LAN to the Internet.

Protocol(s) Supported   Like the network devices in a LAN, routers support specific data transmission protocols, such as TCP/IP or the Novell protocol IPX/SPX. Note which protocols are supported by any routers you have installed.

Speed   The speed of a WAN is determined by speed of the wide area communications links, not by the speed of the LANs those links are connecting. This is because the communications links are much slower than LANs. A typical LAN speed is 10 million bits per second. A T1 line, considered to be a large wide area communications link, transfers data at only the rate of 1.5 million bits per second. Note the speeds of the links in your WAN in Part 3 of Workform F.

BANDWIDTH TO ISP

Single-building libraries and libraries with branches but no local system may also have wide area connections installed. Most often these connections are to the Internet. The connections may be established as needed through a modem and phone line at each PC, or they may be permanent connections through a dedicated telephone line between the library and its Internet service provider (ISP). The speed of a dial-up connection is the speed of the slowest of the two modems used to establish the connection. The speed of a dedicated line to an ISP is the speed of the communications link, typically 56K or T1.

Part 4: Staff Skills

In this section you will be recording your assessment of the computer skill levels of your staff. Most of the technology products you will be considering in your planning process have been developed to operate on PCs. The dominant user interface for PCs is the graphical user interface of Microsoft's Windows. (The user interface controls how a person interacts with a computer program.) The advantage of a standard user interface like Windows is that computer programs, also called "applications," can be written to interact with the user in a consistent way, lessening the amount of time it takes a user to learn to operate a new program.

Windows Skills

Fewer than 50 percent of American households had personal computers in 1996; staff members who don't have PCs at home and haven't used them at work may not be familiar with the basic features and operations of Windows. However, to use many of the products you will be choosing in this process, a basic understanding of Windows will be necessary. If your staff doesn't have Windows skills, you will need to plan for training.

Use Part 4 of Workform F to record your estimate of the number of staff in your library who have no experience with Windows, the number of staff who have limited experience, and those with a high level of Windows skills who are comfortable and confident in their use of PCs with Windows.

Web-Browser Skills

The other user interface that is becoming as important as Windows is the World Wide Web browser. The browser is a common interface for a wide variety of information products, particularly those that are accessed through the Internet. Web browsers have much in common with Windows, but they also have unique features, including hypertext links, the ability to launch helper applications, and bookmark files, among other things. In today's libraries, browser skills are as important as Windows skills. You need to determine the number of staff in your library with browser skills as well. Again, identify the number of staff with no experience, those with limited experience, and staff who have a high level of Web-browser skills.

Applications

You may already have some applications installed on PCs in your library with which some or all of your staff are familiar. Note the names of those applications and the number of staff who are skilled in using them.

Part 5: Public Skills

Every community has people who are comfortable with computers and use them daily at home, work, or school, just as every community has people who have had no exposure to computers due to lack of opportunity or interest. Although all communities have people with widely varying skill levels, some communities will have much higher concentrations than others of people who are computer-literate. In planning to implement technology products that will be used by the public, it is important to assess the general skill level of the population to whom the service will be targeted. Factors to consider when assessing the public skill level include the number of high-tech business and industries in your area, the number of post-secondary schools in the area, and the degree to which the local public schools have incorporated technology in their classrooms.

If you are planning to purchase a technology product to be used in the children's department and all the schools in your service area already have computers in the classrooms, it is reasonable to assume that little or no computer training will be needed for the children to effectively use the product. If your community has a low percentage of households with personal computers, few computer stores, or no local Internet service provider, your target population may need training in basic computer skills before using some products. In evaluating your options and determining resource allocations later in the *Wired for the Future* process, it will be important to include your estimates of the public's computer skills in your assessments.

Completing this section of the form is based solely on "informed guessing." There is no way to develop firm estimates of the actual percentage of the public with specific levels of computer skills unless your service population is so small you know everyone in town.

Part 6: Technical Staff Skills

As you integrate technology into your library operations, you will have to provide technical support to keep your software, equipment, and networks operating at full efficiency. At a minimum, you will probably need access to people who can install and configure PCs or network equipment and troubleshoot and repair basic problems with PCs or networks. Depending on your technology plan, you may need access to people with other skills as well.

Complete one copy of Workform F Part 6 for the entire library system. Use the "Skills Needed" column to record the technical support skills that will be needed to implement your plan. Then complete the "Skills Available" section.

If you need more technical support than you currently have, decide where you will get that support and record that information in the "Source of Additional Technical Support (if Required)" column. You have a variety of options. You might choose to train existing staff, or you might choose to hire new staff who already have the skills you need. You may also have access to some of the skills you need from other departments in your city or county government. Finally, you might choose to outsource your technical support by entering into a contract with a local technical support company.

Is Your Building Ready for Computers?

Every new device you decide to add to your library as the result of the technology planning process will have certain facility requirements that must be met. Use a separate copy of Workform G: Facility Review to record your assessments of the readiness of each of your facilities to accommodate new or expanded technology. You will find that each library facility is unique. Workform G provides you with a general outline to record the conditions in your facilities. A description of some of the things you might consider as you complete Workform G follows.

Electricity

All of the equipment you add as a result of your plan will need electricity to operate.

Outlets

You will probably need a minimum of two outlets for each computer, one for the PC and one for the monitor. A bar code reader may require an outlet, too, as will a printer. A CD-ROM tower will require an outlet as well. Note, too, that many technology products include transformers on their power cords. These square "boxes" can often block access to the second outlet of a two-outlet plug simply because of their size.

Circuits

Not only will you need outlets to plug the devices into, you will need sufficient electrical service to your building to support the new equipment. Personal computers draw more power than dumb terminals; you probably can't even do a one-for-one replacement of terminals with PCs without increasing your electrical service. If you have a map of the electrical circuits in your building, study it to determine how much unused capacity you have now. For estimating purposes, assume a PC and its monitor draws five amps of power. Theoretically, each twenty-amp circuit in your building can support four PCs being used simultaneously.

Unless you are an expert electrician, you probably won't be able to determine your electrical capacity without outside assistance. You may need to add more circuits; you may need to have the electric utility bring more service from the power pole to your building. You will probably want to hire an electrician to review your electrical conditions and help you determine what you might need. As you assess your options in Tasks 9 through 12, you will be able to determine more specifically the electrical requirements of the options you are considering. However, it is important that you understand your present conditions and any limitations that exist in your electrical infrastructure before you begin to choose new technology applications.

Cabling

Each device that is to be connected to a local area network will need data cabling to connect it to the network. See the Building Wiring/Data Cabling Tech Note for more information on this topic. Record current conditions.

Lighting

Lighting appropriate for working on computer screens is different from lighting needed at card catalogs or nonautomated desks for staff. At one time it was difficult to find information about lighting requirements, but the explosion of information available on the Internet has changed all that. You can order the latest lighting standards for educational institutions from American National Standards Institute online at http://www.ansi.org/cat_b.html.

Air Conditioning

Each new device you add to your building will generate a little bit of additional heat. If you are adding only a few computers, the increased heat will probably not be noticeable. If you are replacing all of the dumb terminals with high-end personal computers or adding a significant number of new devices to your building, you may very well be taxing the capabilities of your building's air conditioning. Architects and contractors estimate that a PC with a monitor generates as much heat as a person. Can your air conditioning handle the increased load? Your HVAC contractor can help you determine the building's capacity for absorbing increased heat production.

Space

Each piece of equipment you acquire as a result of your technology plan will take up space in your building. New equipment will fill up unused space first. If you have no unused space in your buildings now, new equipment will have to displace items that are currently using space—old equipment, desks, filing cabinets, book stacks, etc. Do a visual survey of your facilities and estimate how many square feet of unused space you have available. Then consider what could be moved or discarded to create additional space if you find that you need it.

To help in evaluating your space requirements later in the planning process, you might want to note on Workform G how much space you currently allocate for the equipment you have installed. For example, if you have six online catalog terminals in a 60-square-foot space, you are allocating 10 square feet per device. As a rule of thumb, you will probably want to allocate a minimum of 9 square feet per terminal or PC workstation.

Furniture

Workstations, terminals, and printers need to be set on furniture, and the furniture that is most functional is specially designed for the equipment. Look at the furniture that is currently holding your equipment. Is it functional? Is it too crowded, or is there room for additional equipment on your existing furniture? Might you be able to replace old furniture that takes up a lot of space with new furniture that is more space-efficient?

You can find listings for dozens of furniture suppliers on the Internet, a number of whom specialize in library furniture. In some cases, these suppliers have online catalogs; in others, you can request that a catalog be sent to you. One comprehensive listing of furniture suppliers that includes listings for library suppliers can be found at http://www.workspace-resources.com/2mfr_b.htm. When you are looking for furniture, remember to consider the needs of people in wheelchairs.

How Can You Use All of This Data?

When you finish Workforms F and G you will have a lot of detailed information about your current conditions. Workform H: SWOT (strengths, weaknesses, opportunities, and threats) Analysis of the Library Technology Environment will help you put this information into a planning context to identify the major strengths and weaknesses in your current infrastructure and to identify any threats or opportunities in the library, the community, or the field of technology itself that might affect the library's planning process. To do this, first review the information on Workforms F and G and look for areas of strength and weakness. It may be that while your current hardware is outdated (a weakness), your staff is very enthusiastic about technology and is looking forward to having access to the new hardware and software (a strength). Use this as an opportunity to really consider what all of the detailed information means.

When you have finished compiling your strengths and weaknesses on Workform H, spend some time talking about any pending or future threats or opportunities that might have an impact on the library's technology planning. These can come from the external environment or from within the library. For example, threats from the external environment might include budget restrictions, community concerns about pornography on the Internet, or lack of a local Internet service provider (ISP). Threats from within the library might include staff resistance to technology or lack of agreement on service priorities. External opportunities might include strong support for technology development from city or county government leaders or financial support from local businesses and industry. Internal opportunities can be as diverse as a new library board chair who strongly supports technology to a building or remodeling program that will allow you to update your electrical system. At the conclusion of the SWOT analysis you should have a concise overview of your current technology infrastructure and a clear sense of your planning environment.

NOTES

1. Ethel Himmel and William James Wilson, *Planning for Results: A Public Library Transformation Process* (Chicago: ALA, 1998).
2. Charles McClure and others, *Planning and Role-Setting for Public Libraries* (Chicago: ALA, 1987).
3. Himmel and Wilson.
4. Himmel and Wilson, 28.

Chapter 3

Discovering Options

MILESTONES

By the time you complete this chapter you should

- know where to find information about products/services that support your activities

- know what elements to consider when reviewing technology applications

- know what to look for when comparing the potential effectiveness of your options

Learning and Keeping Current

Everyone working in libraries today is a part of the technological revolution whether they want to be or not. Technology is an integral part of the way information is created and disseminated and public libraries are, first and foremost, information places. Therefore, library professionals have a vested interest in understanding today's technology and being able to predict where the technologies that will affect libraries will go tomorrow or next year.

Certainly, everyone involved in this planning process has to understand the wide variety of options that are open to the library before they can make decisions about the best technology infrastructure and products to achieve the library's desired outcomes. The two tasks you need to accomplish the Discovering Options step are

TASK 7
Become Familiar with Current Technologies and
Developing Trends

TASK 8
Evaluate the Options for Your Highest Priority Activities

TASK 7
Become Familiar with Current Technologies and Developing Trends

In this task you will be introduced to a wide variety of sources of information about technology-based products and services. Using those sources, you will begin to gather a common set of information about possible technology-based products and services to support your activities.

Who is responsible for Task 7?
The committee chairperson will lead this activity.

Who else is involved in Task 7?
All of the committee members will be involved in researching and discussing options.

What data is needed for Task 7?
You will need the prioritized list of activities you completed in Task 5: Determine Which Activities Require Technology-Based Solutions.

What workforms are used in Task 7?

Workform D: Library Technology Needs Summary
Workform I: Product/Service Options

What outside assistance would be helpful in Task 7?

This is a task in which outside assistance might be very helpful. The committee might want to ask staff members or others with special expertise to make short presentations or present demonstrations.

How long will Task 7 take?

The research element of this task started during the orientation process at the first meeting of the committee and will continue throughout the planning process and after. The discussion of what has been learned will occur during one or two meetings. The number of meetings will depend on whether outside assistance is used.

Where Do You Start Learning about Your Options?

In chapter 2, Identifying Technology Needs, you reviewed your current library service plan and developed a list of activities that could be accomplished using technology. Those activities were recorded in priority order on Workform D: Library Technology Needs Summary along with the ways your library will measure the impact of the activity on helping the library reach its goals. Now you need to become familiar with the product and service options that are currently available to support your activities as well as the options that might become available in the near future.

Start by listing each of your activities on a separate copy of Workform I: Product/Service Options. Photocopy the forms and give copies to each member of the committee and any others who are helping you identify your options. Then, as each of you identifies a possible product or service for one of those activities, use the form to record information about the product or service. You may need only one form for some activities. For others, you may need five or six copies. This, obviously, will depend on the number of technology-based products or services available (or soon to be available) that would support the activity.

Although you are looking for specific information about products and services, don't focus your attention too narrowly. As you work through this task, you should also be developing a broad general understanding of library technology applications, implications, and trends. This framework will be invaluable to you when you begin to make decisions later in this process.

Where Can You Find Information about Various Products and Services?

The first challenge you face in identifying your options is finding out what products or services exist now or may soon become available. This means you need to make a conscious and continuous effort to stay abreast of developing technologies—and this is not a one-time event. Even after you have developed your technology plan, you will have a continuing need to stay aware of changes in library technology. Because technology changes constantly, you will want to confirm your decisions at each stage of your plan's implementation. You can do that only if you have kept current with the changing environment.

Keeping up with technology trends is not a one-person process either. Technology is so integrated with the basic services in most libraries that everyone uses it and every service is affected by it in one way or another. Everyone in your library who participates in the selection of materials or the design and delivery of public services should be responsible for keeping up with available technology products in his or her area of expertise. You expect your staff to bring a great new book or periodical title to a selector's attention if they hear of it; the same should be true for technology products.

Whatever the difficulties librarians may have in keeping up with current technologies and developing trends, lack of information is not among them. We are all surrounded by vast amounts of information about technology in the popular press, in library literature, on television, and through the Internet itself. As a matter of fact, there is so much information available that it is often difficult to find what you need. At one time or another you have probably felt like the woman who typed a request into an Internet search engine and got 12,350 hits. She didn't want 12,350 hits—she wanted the one right answer!

While there may be no such thing as "one right answer" to your technology needs, there are a number of ways that you can find specific information about current technologies as well as identify and track future trends. They include reading library and technology journals and books; talking to other librarians, information professionals, and technology experts; attending conference programs; visiting conference exhibits, computer shows, or computer stores to try new technologies; attending formal training programs or classes; and exploring the Internet.

Read Many librarians are still more comfortable learning from the printed word than the computer screen. Fortunately, there are hundreds of print resources available on all aspects of technology, including adaptive technology for people with disabilities. Magazines and journals usually provide the most-current information on issues and topics. Certainly, public library professionals should read major library publications including *Library Journal, American Libraries,* and

Public Libraries, all of which routinely carry stories and news bulletins about library technology issues. Journals that deal specifically with library technology include *Library Hi-Tech, Computers in Libraries,* and *Information Technology and Libraries.* Journals that deal with electronic databases and reference tools include *Information Today, Searcher,* and *Online.* Finally, journals such as *Library Trends* explore the future of libraries, including the impact of technology.

In addition, dozens of technology magazines exist, many of them with a very narrow focus. Some magazines are devoted to Microsoft Windows, to interesting WWW sites, to computer gaming, to portable computing, to Macintosh computers, and to PCs. Issues in developing and managing networks are covered in *Network, LAN Times,* and *InfoWorld,* all of which have electronic editions on the Internet as well as print versions. In fact, it is likely that you can find a magazine about almost any aspect of computing that interests you. The Internet search engine Yahoo at www.yahoo.com provides an index to many of these technology magazines. A number of more-general technology magazines, including *Wired,* provide an overview of technology issues, identify trends, and help readers understand how various technologies interrelate. Finally, mainstream magazines, from *The New Yorker* to *People,* regularly include information about how current technologies are affecting people's lives. Because they are written for the layperson and often include a context for the information they provide, these articles can be very helpful for getting a sense of the bigger picture.

Books can provide a more in-depth look at technology. Check out any bookstore and you will find aisles of new books on all aspects of technology, from scholarly tomes on the impact of technology on society to specific how-to manuals for popular software programs. Titles are devoted to adaptive technology for people with disabilities as well as adaptive technology in libraries. Your library collection probably includes the best of these resources as well. In addition to these general books, reports from specific studies that have looked at the impact of technology on libraries contain valuable information for librarians. You will find citations to new and important reports in the library journals mentioned previously. Two examples of this type of report are the *Buildings, Books, and Bytes: Libraries and Communities in the Digital Age* and *The 1997 National Survey of U.S. Public Libraries and the Internet.*[1]

Many of the traditional review sources for the selection of library materials have expanded their coverage to include electronic resources. These reviews focus solely on evaluating the content of the resource, and little information is given on the hardware and software needed to support the product, other than the operating system under which it runs. For products you intend to make available using the library's hardware, as opposed to products you acquire for circulation, you need to determine this information as well. Much of the information can be gathered from product literature produced by the vendor or from phone calls to the vendor. Sometimes the technical requirements to support a product can be found on a vendor's Web page. The 101 Micro Series from ALA also provides detailed reviews including costs, hardware requirements, and additional software needed for various products.[2]

Talk   Librarians are among the most helpful people around, and they are used to answering questions. After all, that is what they do for a living. In your search for current information and when you attempt to identify future trends, you will probably find that your colleagues are extremely helpful. As you think about your colleagues, don't be parochial. Libraries of all types are incorporating technology into their ongoing operations. It may be that the experiences your local school librarians have had assisting students to use the Internet will be helpful to you or your staff as you plan for providing public access to the Internet. Your local college librarians may have experience with online databases that you haven't used. Even staff from libraries that are not as technologically advanced as your library may have things to teach you. If they are buying new hardware or software, they have probably spent a lot of time evaluating their various options. You can use the results of their studies to update your own information about current conditions.

You are not limited to talking to librarians who work with or near you. There are hundreds of electronic discussion groups (discussion lists) on every aspect of technology and on every aspect of public libraries as well. At present, PUBLIB (www.sunsite.berkeley.edu/publib) is the oldest and most popular national discussion list for public librarians, and it regularly addresses a broad range of public library issues including those surrounding technology. Most states also have statewide library discussion lists that address similar topics. There are also discussion lists for librarians interested in discussing adaptive technology such as ADAPT-L for people with disabilities. All of these discussion lists are essentially electronic conversations. They work like e-mail, but instead of sending your message to one recipient you send it to all of the subscribers to the discussion list. The recipients can then respond to you directly or to the entire list.

Two excellent resources for locating discussion lists on subjects of interest to you are *Liszt, The Mailing List Directory* (http://www.liszt.com) and *Tile.Net/ Lists: The Comprehensive Internet Reference to Discussion Lists* (http://www.tile.net/tile/ listserv). *Liszt* provides information about more than 120 discussion lists on some aspect of librarianship and almost 150 discussion lists on computers. *Tile.Net* has more than 120 discussion lists on libraries, 184 on computers, and more than 140 on the Internet. Both directories can be searched by subject, and both include the information you need to subscribe to the list or lists of your choice. *Liszt* also has a helpful document called Tips for Newcomers that you might want to read if you have never joined a discussion list before.

No matter how small your community is, you will find that technical experts are available to you locally. Make friends with your city or county information systems staff. They make decisions that will affect library operations and can be a wonderful source of information about the big picture. The more they know about the library and its technology needs, the more likely they are to make decisions that will be advantageous to you.

Local computer user groups can be another source of information and assistance. If you are planning to provide public access to the Internet, you may want to get these people involved to help provide assistance to the public. They may also be able to give you information about expected product enhancements as well as tips and tools for using products more effectively.

Finally, talk to sales and vendor representatives from library automation firms. Naturally, they will be presenting their information in the context of their own products. However, most vendor representatives are very knowledgeable about the field of library automation and can provide you with excellent insights into what the near future might bring.

Attend Programs at Meetings or Conferences

Library associations at the local, state, regional, and national levels all present regular conferences with programs designed to keep working librarians informed about all aspects of the profession. Your local and state conferences probably include panels of working librarians talking about how they have addressed technology problems that you may be currently facing. These conferences often feature a nationally recognized automation expert to provide an overview of the current technology along with forecasts about the future. Regional and national conferences also include panels of working librarians, but rather than speaking from the perspective of a single state, these panelists provide a mix of ideas from around the country. These larger conferences normally feature more technology experts, as well. For example, if you attend the American Library Association annual conference, held in late June each year, you will have the opportunity to hear many of the leaders in library automation as well as technology experts from other fields. The Public Library Association (PLA) national conference, held every two years in the spring, focuses on programs of specific interest to public librarians and always features discussions of the latest technologies and their impact on public libraries. The Library Information and Technology Association (LITA) also periodically presents national conferences and regional institutes that are focused solely on the technology affecting libraries. Other specialty professional conferences include the annual National Online Meeting or the Integrated Online Library Systems conference.

Your conference attendance does not have to be restricted to library-specific conferences. There are thousands of technology conferences held around the world each year. The Tech Calendar (http://www.techweb.com/calendar) provides a complete listing of these conferences divided by month, location, or subject. The subjects are grouped by categories; for instance, the Internet/ online category is subdivided by electronic commerce, Internet, intranet, and Java. The computing industry category includes career development opportunities, computer industry research, computer manufacturing, computer sales and distribution, computers in the community, human factors, intellectual property, regulatory, and venture. Each of the subject listings includes multiple conference listings. You might want to check out the conferences in your area to see if any of them include topics that will affect your library. For example, it seems likely that conferences on computers in the community and intellectual property would include programs of real value to professional librarians.

Look at and Try Technologies

Library and technology conferences offer more than just an opportunity to attend programs and hear experts. Most conferences also include exhibit areas where vendors display their latest hardware and software. You can actually try out these new products with someone available to answer all of your questions. You can also compare and contrast the products of several different vendors to determine which best meets the needs of your library.

You don't have to wait for conference exhibits to try out new products. A number of products are available as demonstration files, either from CD-ROMs that you can request from the vendor or via a download from a Web site. *Computers in Libraries* publishes an annual buyer's guide issue that includes contact information for many of the vendors of library-oriented products, and in 1997 the *Library Journal* began an annual review of database suppliers in its May issue to supplement *LJ*'s regular column on electronic resources. Library automation vendors' user group meetings often include demonstrations by suppliers of add-on products as well.

Your local computer store has a variety of equipment available for you to try and an experienced sales staff to answer your questions. You can also visit other libraries that have purchased the equipment or software that you are considering and see for yourself how it is working. The vendor in question should be able to give you a list of clients near you. Finally, you can invite vendors to come to your library to give you an onsite demonstration of their products. This will give you a chance to involve more people in the demonstration and to compare and contrast several products.

Attend Workshops or Classes

As you install various equipment and use multiple software applications, you are going to reach the point where you need specific help operating the equipment or using the software program. You can work with the technical manuals that came with the equipment or software and with the help programs that came with the software, but that may be not be enough. At that point, you may want to consider attending a workshop or taking a class on the subject. For example, it seems clear now that most PCs are going to continue to operate in a Windows mode for the foreseeable future. Therefore, to work effectively with PCs you are going to have to understand how Windows works. If you are confused by icons, maximizing, minimizing, files, documents, and notepads and you're not quite sure what the desktop is, you would benefit from attending an introductory Windows workshop. These are offered by many computer stores as well as by private computer training companies and many community colleges. If you live in a community with no computer stores or community colleges, you may be able to hire one of the computer teachers from the high school (or one of the high school students themselves) to tutor you or to present a class for you and the rest of the library staff on Windows basics. Classes and workshops on other applications are widely available from both commercial providers and community colleges.

Also, a wide variety of video and CD-ROM training aids are available to you. These can provide you with everything from an overview of spreadsheets to step-by-step instructions on how to operate a specific program. This type of training allows you to learn at your own pace and is available for a quick review if you forget how to do something. The training can be scheduled at your convenience, and the training tools can be used by more than one person, which may make them more cost-effective than formal classes or workshops. However, remember that software is upgraded regularly. Be sure that any video or CD-ROM training product you purchase is for exactly the same software or hardware that you are using.

Explore the Internet

The Internet contains an astonishing treasure trove of information. If you want to know something about any aspect of technology, the chances are excellent you can find it somewhere in cyberspace. A number of regularly published electronic journals will keep you up-to-date with the latest technology news. You can also use one or more of the Internet search engines to find the information you need. Windweaver's Search Guide (http://www.windweaver. com/searchguide.htm) provides a very clear overview of the various search engines and some useful preliminary searching hints. In a relatively brief time the Internet has become an integral part of library operations. With the Internet, like almost everything else, "practice makes perfect." The more you use the Internet, the more you will want to use it.

There are also a number of very useful, authoritative public Web sites that many libraries will want to link to from their own home pages. *Library Journal*'s Web Watch column reviews sites (www.ljdigital.com). The Internet Public Library (www.ipl.org) also finds and links to high-quality public sites. Many local and regional governments, newspapers, and nonprofit community organizations are developing Web pages the local library will want to link to as well. Fortunately, most free-of-charge Web resources can be added to a library's technology environment by adding another link on a Web page. However, don't forget that the more resources you offer at a PC, the longer the average user will be at the workstation, ultimately triggering a need for more PCs or the imposition of time limits on use. Even the most-stable Web links need staff to check them periodically to ensure that the resource hasn't moved or changed. In other words, free Web links aren't really free.

What Do You Look for When Evaluating Possible Products and Services?

In many ways, the process of selecting technology products is similar to the process used to select other library resources. You apply the traditional criteria of scope, authority, timeliness, appropriate presentation level for the intended audience, cost, etc., to the technology products you review. Just as many of the information resources you currently use are available in multiple formats (print, CD-ROM, etc.), so, too, will many of the electronic products you evaluate be available in multiple formats. Possibilities include CD-ROM, online through local loading, or online via the Internet. This means that not only will you need to select the products you want to offer, you will also have to choose the format(s) that will be most effective in your library.

One major difference exists between the selection process used for technology-based products and the selection process you use for print materials. For print products, most librarians choose the "best" book they can find within their price range based on their selection criteria. For technology products, it is often more useful to identify several products and formats that could meet your needs, then select from among them the one that best fits in your own technology environment or infrastructure.

To select among a variety of electronic products and to determine the appropriate formats for those products, you need to consider both the infrastructure requirements of the products and the following characteristics:

- number of sites needing access
- number of users
- location of the users: in-library only, access from off-site, or both
- licensing restrictions on the use of the data
- frequency of updates of the data contained in the resource and the currency of the data
- authentication of users
- indexing and retrieval features
- user interface to the product, including the special interface needs of persons with disabilities
- costs to support the product

- training requirements to support usage of the materials, including training the staff and training the public

Each of these areas is explained more fully in the following sections. Use Workform I to record your findings.

Number of Sites and Users

Some electronic products are designed to be used by one person at a time. Many of the popular CD-ROM products marketed for the home user are designed this way. Including these products in a circulating collection, or circulating them to one user at a time for in-house use is fine, but these products cannot be made accessible to multiple users or multiple sites over a network because of licensing restrictions. If you are considering replacing a print encyclopedia with an encyclopedia on CD-ROM, or if you are planning to subscribe to a number of full-text magazine titles on CD-ROM, think about the number of simultaneous users the print versions of these products typically support. If your library often has people working with multiple volumes of the encyclopedia at the same time, a CD-ROM with a single-user license will reduce the availability of your service because only one person will be able to use the encyclopedia at a time.

Location of the User

The location of the expected user is another key element in deciding among various products and formats. Print materials are easily perused only by people with physical access to the material. Materials installed on a LAN, such as CD-ROMs or data from CD-ROMs loaded onto a server's hard drives, are often restricted by licensing to exclude use outside a library's facilities. Internet resources that are licensed by commercial suppliers may be restricted to use from specific computers based on the computers' network addresses. This means that a library seeking to provide service seven days a week, twenty-four hours a day, via dial-in or the Internet, may find that certain of its electronic materials are not available to off-site users. If "7 × 24" service is key to your goals, it needs to be part of the criteria for evaluating products.

Licensing Restrictions

If you decide to enter into a licensing agreement for electronic resources that can be used by more than one user at a time, you will find that there are a number of ways vendors license their products. Licensing on a per-site or per-simultaneous-user basis is common. Per-site licensing generally allows access to the database from any workstation on a LAN. Each LAN, even if linked by a WAN, is considered a separate site.

If you purchase your license on a per-simultaneous-user basis, each user adds to the cost of the product or service. Therefore, you want to correlate the number of licenses you purchase with the usage you anticipate. If you purchase too many licenses, you waste money because you are paying for access your customers never use. On the other hand, too few licenses will frustrate your staff and public because they will be turned away from using the information, just like continually getting a busy signal when trying to make a phone call. Although you obviously want to make your initial estimates of the number of simultaneous users as accurate as possible, remember that you can adjust those estimates later. Some vendors or network license monitoring software can offer you regular usage reports identifying how frequently a user was denied access because the license restrictions had been reached. Reports such as these can help you determine if you have too few licenses to meet your demand.

Other common licensing agreements include unlimited use by authorized users and pay-per-use options, in which you license the right to access a particular resource a specific number of times. Before you can enter into a licensing agreement for networked resources, you will need to decide the number of sites or library locations in which you plan to offer the product, and you will need to estimate the expected number of simultaneous users.

Frequency of Updates and Currency of Data

Consider if the timeliness of the data is crucial to your customers when evaluating formats for your library. The frequency with which information can be updated is a major advantage of electronic resources, especially Internet-based resources. Indexes to time-sensitive materials such as newspapers, magazines, or investment services, and the materials themselves, can be updated daily or, if news is breaking fast, even more frequently. Information output to a physical medium, such as print or CD-ROM, is slower due to the production and shipping time.

Consider, too, how current the data is when the product is updated. The production cycles for some physical media require cutoff dates for included data well in advance of the production date. The product may be updated monthly, but the information incorporated each month may, itself, be a month old at that point.

Authentication of Users

Some vendors offer authentication options that permit a library to "authorize" an off-site user's access to remote resources. This is done through an interaction between the database vendor's system and the library's local system at the start of a requested session, but it requires that the library have an accessible patron database that can be used as the basis of authentication.

Vendors who offer unlimited-access licenses to resources will often require some form of patron authentication as a condition of their licenses as well.

Indexing and Retrieval Features

User-appropriate indexing and retrieval interfaces are as important in electronic resources as they are in traditional print resources. Some products have different retrieval options in each available format. The print and CD-ROM formats may both use controlled vocabulary indexing, although the CD-ROM may offer multifield Boolean searching as well. The Internet version of the same product may rely solely on the full-text retrieval capabilities of an electronic search engine, such as Excite or AltaVista.

The best way to evaluate the indexing and retrieval of various formats of a product or various products is to develop a set of sample searches and perform them on all of the products and formats you are evaluating. Note the differences in the responses retrieved. You may want to perform the same search several times on the same product and note whether there are any inconsistencies in the responses you receive.

When evaluating indexing, think also about who will be using the product and whether they will have access to a staff member to answer questions if necessary. Complex retrieval options often require professional help to be used effectively; if you are choosing "self-service" products, a simpler indexing interface may be better.

User Interface

Many products are available with multiple user interfaces. A vendor's CD-ROM product, typically, will require you to load proprietary client software on each workstation that will be accessing the product. That same vendor's product mounted on the World Wide Web will be accessible with any standard Web browser. The vendor may also offer a Z39.50 interface that will permit you to access the data with Z39.50 client software. (See the Tech Notes for more on Z39.50). Many library automation system vendors imbed Z39.50 client functionality in their online catalog clients; this means your customers can access the data using the same interface they use for your online catalog.

The user interface you choose will have an impact on the costs to support the product. Loading and maintaining proprietary clients on each public and staff workstation will be time consuming. If you are already using your library automation system vendor's online catalog client or a Web browser to access other electronic resources, you can extend the use of that software to a new product rather than adding another software package you will have to support.

If you do not provide adaptive technology for people with disabilities, then you will want to consider how you will plan to do so. For example, library users who are visually impaired may need a special large-print interface or an interface that reads aloud the text on the screen.

Training Requirements

The products and formats you consider will have differing staff and public training requirements as well. Materials loaded on your library automation system may be accessible from the same user interface as your online catalog, which would make them relatively easy for the staff and public to use. A collection of different databases that are accessible through a single-user interface because they came from a single supplier, such as SilverPlatter or Ovid, will obviously require less training than a variety of databases, each with a different interface and search mechanism. However, be aware that you may sacrifice some product-specific retrieval features to achieve this training cost reduction. Web-based products tend to look the same on the surface because of the common browser-based interface, but they are usually very dissimilar in indexing and retrieval options. A novice user may find them easy to use at first encounter, but to truly get the most from the product, staff training will be essential and public training will be quite useful.

Cost to Support the Product

Even if a vendor offers all of the various formats of a product for the same price, the costs to support the formats are rarely the same. Print products or single-user CD-ROMs must be duplicated to be accessible at multiple sites. LAN-based products require a network and sufficient storage and processor power to make the products available to the number of users licensed to access them; they will also require staff time to load updates to the data and the software. Products accessed from the Internet must have telecommunications connections to devices in the library and enough bandwidth to be retrievable with acceptable response time. Both local and remotely accessible networked resources require user workstations configured with the necessary hardware and software to retrieve and display the data.

TASK 8
Evaluate the Options for Your Highest Priority Activities

In this task you will select the products and services that will be used in Tasks 9 through 12 to determine your proposed technology infrastructure. To do this, you will be working with your highest priority activities and the products and services that support them. You will use the measures of success for those activities to determine which of the product/service options you have discovered will be most likely to produce your desired outcomes.

Who is responsible for Task 8?

The committee chair will lead this task.

Who else is involved in Task 8?

All members of the committee will be involved in reviewing these products and determining which would be most likely to produce the desired outcomes.

What data is needed for Task 8?

All of the information you need is on your completed copies of Workforms D and I.

What workforms are used in Task 8?

Workform D: Library Technology Needs Summary
Workform I: Product/Service Options
Workform J: Product Review

What outside assistance would be helpful in Task 8?

As in Task 7, it is likely that outside assistance will be helpful here. You may even want to consider forming several subcommittees, each of which would be responsible for evaluating options for one or more activities. In this case, you want to include at least one member of the planning committee on each subcommittee.

How long will Task 8 take?

If you have subcommittees working on this task, you will need to schedule time for each of them to meet. The planning committee can complete this task in a single meeting.

Why Work with Only Your Highest Priority Activities in This Task?

As you have no doubt discovered, there are a seemingly endless number of technology-based services and products available—and more are becoming available each day. When all of the committee members have completed Task 7, you are going to end up with a large stack of options requiring a number of different infrastructure investments. The challenge you now face is selecting from among those options. This would be difficult even if you had all of the money you needed to develop and maintain all of the technology infrastructures required to support your preferred options. However, for most libraries, financial restraints will require that you select from among the available infrastructures as well as from among the available products and services. What this means is that you are now facing the classic question of the chicken or the egg—which comes first? Obviously, the infrastructure choices you make will affect your product choices, but how do you select an infrastructure without knowing what products or services you want it to support?

You should use a few of your highest priority activities as a foundation for determining a proposed technology infrastructure. This will ensure that the decisions you are making will result in achieving those outcomes that were identified as the most important in your library service plan. Once you have determined the most effective infrastructure to support your highest priority activities, you can select other products and services from among those supported by the same infrastructure. Then, if you have sufficient resources, you may be able to enhance your primary infrastructure to support other products and services that would be nice to have but that are less critical to your success.

You will start this task by referring back to Workform D: Library Technology Needs Summary to identify the three activities that had the highest priority. Write those three activities in the boxes labeled Activity 1, Activity 2, and Activity 3 on Workform J: Product Review.

Next, separate all of the copies of Workform I: Product/Service Options that relate to those three activities. (Put the other copies of Workform I to one side, you will need them again in Task 12: Select the Products and Services That Use the Approved Infrastructure.) *Note:* You will be using only the copies of Workform I that relate to your highest three activities for the remainder of this task and in Task 9: Identify a Proposed Technology Infrastructure.

How Do You Identify a Product or Service as a Viable Option?

As you look at the options you have identified for your three highest priority activities, you will see that although the products may be similar, each seems to have its own special twist and comparing all of the available options can be very confusing. How, then, is the committee supposed to make sense of all of the possible options available?

You begin the evaluation of your options with a review of your desired results. A product that can be accessed by only one user at a time is of no use to you if you have already determined that you will measure your success by the number of simultaneous users of a service. It doesn't matter if the single-user product is critically acclaimed—it doesn't meet your needs.

Therefore, before you can begin to select from all of the available technical products and services, you need to identify the general characteristics that will be important in any of the options you might consider for each activity. To do this, go back again to Workform D: Library Technology Needs Summary. This workform includes the measures you plan to use to evaluate the impact of each of your technology-based activities. Use the measure or measures associated with each activity to identify the characteristics that you will look for in a technology-based product or service you select to support this activity.

Let's go back to the example of a business goal used earlier. One activity that might support the goal was "subscribe to a wide variety of business periodicals." In the example, the objective that relates to this activity was "At least 75 percent of the small business owners in Anytown who reported that they used the library to find business-related information in the past year will say that information was available to them in a convenient location." The underlying measure in this objective is convenience. Therefore, any options you consider to provide access to a wide variety of business periodicals should provide access from more than one site and to more than one user.

Workform J: Product Review provides a place for you to indicate the most important characteristics for each of your three highest priority activities. Use measures on Workform D as the basis for your discussion about the most important characteristics for each activity. These characteristics might include access in multiple sites, access by simultaneous users, frequency of data updates, offsite access, currency, ease of use, etc. Remember that each of your technology-related activities can probably be accomplished in several different ways. Keeping this list of characteristics in mind while you consider your options will help you look at all of the available alternatives.

To continue with the business goal example, you could provide access to business periodicals by licensing access to indexes and the full text of a selection of business titles from an Internet site or by licensing a CD-ROM product with the indexes and the full text of those same periodicals. If you choose the CD-ROM option, you could license the CD-ROM for a single user or for multiple simultaneous users over a local area network.

These examples involve selecting a new product to introduce a new service, but instead you may need to focus on upgrading or extending an existing service for your users. In this case, if you already have business periodicals and their indexes available to the users of your central library, you may want to extend that service to include your branches as well. The options for these activities won't require evaluating an information product—you already have the information product; the options for these activities will focus on the infrastructure investments you will need to make.

Whether you are adding a product or expanding a service, your choices will be influenced by the required characteristics you have identified on Workform J, which in turn were based on the desired impact of the activity toward helping the library reach its goals.

How does the desired impact affect your available choices? To make those periodicals available at the branches, one option is to buy another copy of the CD-ROM product for each of the branches. This branch copy could either be a single-user product or a multiuser product on a LAN, depending on the service characteristics you defined as important. Perhaps in a small branch a single-user option would be sufficient, while a larger branch might need a multiuser license, a CD server, and a local area network to serve the expected demand. Other options might be to expand the user licenses for the CD-ROM at the central library and provide access to it by adding a dial-in capability or by installing or expanding dedicated telecommunications links between the central library and the branches. Yet another option is to replace the CD-ROM completely by licensing access to the periodicals from a remote site over the Internet.

Each of these options will support your planned activity; each of these options will help you progress toward achieving your goal. Each option will also have a different set of infrastructure requirements you will need to meet to support the option.

Identifying multiple options to support each activity will give you flexibility in developing your technology plan. There are no right answers or best solutions that will meet the needs of every public library. The goal of technology planning is to identify the options that meet needs in the context of each library's technology environment. Each library has a different set of goals, existing technology, and staff skills on which to build, and each will choose from the options differently based on these factors.

Remember, at this point you have *not* made a decision about the library's infrastructure requirement. Be sure to consider all of the formats available when you are evaluating new products. Unfortunately, libraries too often begin the process of identifying options by first selecting a technology infrastructure and then searching for products that use that infrastructure. For example, a library might first decide to install a CD network, and then begin looking for products it can offer using that network. This approach can seriously limit the number of products from which you can choose.

Of course, some libraries have already made a significant investment in their technical infrastructure and are looking for new ways to increase their usage of that infrastructure. For these libraries, focusing on product options for each activity that make use of the existing infrastructure makes some sense. Keep in mind, however, that the technology products used as components of infrastructure, like network equipment and telecommunications options, are even more volatile than the options for some information products. Just as you are never "done buying books," you will never complete your technical infrastructure. It will need to evolve and be upgraded as technology and information products evolve. As an example, many libraries that bought their first automation system in the 1970s have already replaced the data cabling in the buildings two or three times. If you decide to limit your product options in this planning process to only those products that fit your existing infrastructure, be sure that someone on your staff is scanning the horizon for developing technologies that will have an impact on that infrastructure.

Don't reject options at this stage because you think they are too expensive or because you don't have the technical expertise to implement them.

You may find at later steps in the process that many of your preferred options share a common set of technical or staff-training requirements. An infrastructure investment that might be too expensive to support a single activity could seem reasonable if it helped the library to meet a number of different goals.

How Do You Tentatively Select Your Best Options?

You have used Workform J to indicate the relative importance of the characteristics of the products and/or services that could be used to support your three highest priority activities. Now you will evaluate each of those products or services based on those characteristics. Still using Workform J, list all of the possible products or services you identified for each activity in the rows labeled Option 1, Option 2, etc. (The products/services will be found on Workform I.) If you have identified more than five options, use a second sheet.

Next, you will evaluate each of your options. Using the information about the product or service from Workform I, indicate how closely the product/service matches each of the characteristics. When you complete the review of all of the products/services that might support the activity, you will have all of the information you need for tentative selection of your best choice. The product or service that most closely matches your desired characteristics is your best choice for this activity. When you have selected your best choice for all three of your highest-priority activities, you are ready to move on to Task 9: Identify a Proposed Technology Infrastructure.

NOTES

1. Benton Foundation, *Buildings, Books, and Bytes* (Nov. 1996), available: http://www.benton.org/Library/Kellogg/buildings.htm, Mar. 1998; John Carlo Bertot, Charles McClure, and Patricia Fletcher, *The 1997 National Survey of U.S. Public Libraries and the Internet* (Washington, D.C.: U.S. National Commission on Libraries and Information Science, 1997), summary available: http://www.ala.org/oitp/research/plcon97sum/, Mar. 1998.

2. Patrick R. Dewey, *101 Desktop Publishing and Graphics Programs* (Chicago: ALA, 1993); Patrick R. Dewey, *303 CD-ROMs to Use in Your Library: Descriptions, Evaluations, and Practical Advice* (Chicago: ALA, 1996); Patrick R. Dewey, *303 Software Programs to Use in Your Library: Descriptions, Evaluations, and Practical Advice* (Chicago: ALA, 1998).

Chapter 4

Selecting a Technology Infrastructure and Identifying Products and Services

MILESTONES

By the time you have finished this chapter you should

- understand how to determine your infrastructure requirements

- know how to identify the one-time and ongoing costs of a proposed infrastructure

- understand what to look for when selecting technology vendors

- know how to select products and services that use the infrastructure you select

Making Decisions

In the last two chapters you have gathered data about your library facility, current technology infrastructure, and library service plan along with the many products and services that are available to help you reach your desired outcomes. In this chapter you will use all of that data to determine a technology infrastructure that will support those products and services, identify what you need to implement that infrastructure, and calculate how much it will cost. You will present this proposed infrastructure to the library director and library board for preliminary approval. You will then identify and select products and services that use that infrastructure to accomplish those of your activities that require technology-based solutions. Finally, you will group any activities requiring technology-based solutions that can't be accomplished using your proposed infrastructure and go through this process again to identify additional elements you might want to add to the proposed infrastructure.

The five tasks in Selecting a Technology Infrastructure and Identifying Products and Services are

> TASK 9
> Identify a Proposed Technology Infrastructure
>
> TASK 10
> Determine What It Will Cost to Implement the Proposed Infrastructure
>
> TASK 11
> Obtain Preliminary Approval for the Proposed Infrastructure
>
> TASK 12
> Select the Products and Services That Use the Approved Infrastructure
>
> TASK 13
> Group the Remaining Activities and Begin Again at Task 8.

TASK 9
Identify a Proposed Technology Infrastructure

In this task you will review the infrastructure requirements of the options you tentatively selected in Task 8. Based on those requirements, you will develop a primary technology infrastructure to propose.

Who is responsible for Task 9?
The planning committee chair will lead this task.

Who else is involved in Task 9?

The planning committee will complete the review and make the recommendations.

What data is needed for Task 9?

All of the required information is on Workforms I through M.

What workforms are used in Task 9?

Workform I: Product/Service Options
Workform J: Product Review
Workform K: Infrastructure Evaluation
Workform L: Network Decision Tree
Workform M: Infrastructure Requirements Comparison
Workform N: Gap Analysis

What outside assistance would be helpful in Task 9?

You might want to ask staff members with technical expertise or one of the outside experts listed in Task 1: Determine Your Planning Process to help complete Workform K.

> *Enhanced level of effort:* You could hire an outside consultant to complete this task for you. The committee could then review the consultant's work and revise it as needed.

How long will Task 9 take?

The identification of the infrastructure requirements for your options is the most time-consuming part of this task. The time required to do this will depend on a variety of things including the amount of information you gathered about your options in Task 8 and the number of people involved. When that is done, the comparison of the requirements and selection of a proposed infrastructure can take place in one meeting of the committee.

How Do You Plan for an Infrastructure Investment?

You are basing your technology decisions on the services and programs that you have determined will meet the needs of the people you serve. To do that, you started by developing a prioritized list of your activities (Task 5 and Workforms C, D, and E). Then, focusing on your highest priority activities, you determined the most important characteristics for the product or service option selected to support each activity (Task 8 and Workform I). Next, using those characteristics as your criteria, you identified the information product or service that most closely matched your list of desired characteristics for each activity (Task 8 and Workform J).

Now you are ready to develop a proposed infrastructure. To do that, you will first identify the infrastructure requirements for the three products/services you identified on Workform J: Product Review. Then you will look for common infrastructure requirements among the three products/services. The common requirements will become the basis for your proposed infrastructure. Finally, you will go back to the product/service options listed on Workform I: Product/Service Options and select those that work with the proposed infrastructure.

What Do You Need to Know to Compare the Infrastructure Requirements of Your Best-Choice Options?

For each of the three best-choice options you identified on Workform J: Product Review, you now need to identify the hardware, software, networks, user skills (both staff and public), and technical skills required to implement that option whether that option is a new product or an extension of an existing service.

For example, if you have a CD-ROM database on a stand-alone PC and you wish to make it available to more than one simultaneous user, you need more PCs, a local area network connecting those PCs, and a multiuser license from the CD-ROM supplier. If you want to switch your online catalog's user interface from text-based dumb terminals to a Web browser interface, you need to replace the terminals with PCs that have browser software, install or extend a local area network to connect those PCs to your automation system, and get a license to use your vendor's Web-based catalog. If you have branch libraries, you may also need to upgrade the telecommunications links you use to pass data between the branch libraries and the online system.

Completing Workform K: Infrastructure Evaluation

Use a separate copy of Workform K: Infrastructure Evaluation to record and organize the information you gather about each option. You may want to refer back to the information provided in Task 6 for use with Workform F. Much of that background information given in the instructions for Workform F will be useful in completing Workform K as well. Although Workforms F and K look a lot alike, the kinds of information you are recording on each form are quite different. On Workform F you were recording what you *currently* own, and the data was fairly self-evident. On Workform K you will be considering the elements of the infrastructure you want to put into place, and there are many more issues to consider.

You will complete the Description and Number Needed columns of Workform K for each of your options. The Cost Per Unit and Total Cost columns are optional; they are included here to give you a place to record cost information if you find it as you are researching your infrastructure options. The issues pertaining to costs and information on where to obtain information on costs are discussed in detail in Task 10: Determine What It Will Cost to Implement the Proposed Infrastructure.

Part 1: Client Devices and Software

All client (end-user) devices are connected to a network. For the purposes of this chapter, *client* will mean a client computer or terminal and *server* will mean a server computer. It is assumed that clients are connected to servers by a network. A stand-alone computer used to provide access one user at a time to a database product is considered to be a server on Workform K. A fuller discussion of client/server computing can be found in the Tech Notes.

Client Devices

Character-Based Terminals

Software products have specific requirements for the devices that can be used to deliver and display them. Occasionally, text-based products can be delivered using character-based or "dumb" terminals rather than requiring PCs. If the product you are considering can be delivered with character-based terminals, circle yes on the appropriate line on Workform K.

If terminals can be used, there is generally a requirement that the terminals support a predefined set of rules called "protocols" for interpreting and displaying data. Common terminal protocols in library applications include VT100 and VT420. Be sure to note the necessary terminal protocol on Workform K.

PCs

If the product or service you are considering requires PCs as clients, there are four technical requirements you will need to identify. These include processor type and speed, memory (RAM), available disk space, and operating system.

Processor type means what kind of computer chip is in the machine. The common Intel chips in libraries include 286, 386, 486, and Pentium. Processor speed is a measure of how fast a chip can execute instructions. Processor speeds are expressed in megahertz (MHz).

Random access memory (RAM) is where computers store data being used by the processor. RAM is calculated in megabytes (MB) or gigabytes (GB). Disk storage is where the programs and data are stored when the computer is not using them. Every new program you add to a client machine will require some amount of disk storage on that machine.

Operating System

Software products are written to run under particular operating systems. Programs written for Apple's Mac OS operating system will not run on a machine that has Microsoft's Windows operating system. Some programs written for Windows 95 will not operate on Windows 3.1. Be sure to note the operating system requirements of any product you are considering. In client-server environments, it is possible that the operating system requirements for the client will be different from the operating system requirements of the server.

Color Monitor, Sound Card, and Speakers/Headphones

If you are considering a multimedia product, you may have video display and audio requirements for the client machine as well. A color monitor, a specific type of graphics card, or a specific amount of graphics memory (special memory available on the graphics card or chip) may be required. Often sound cards capable of supporting at least 16-bit sound are necessary as well. If the product requires a sound card, you will need speakers or perhaps headphones for your users.

Speech Synthesizers and Adaptive Keyboards

If you serve people with disabilities, you may need to consider speech synthesis features or adaptive keyboards.

Client Software

Client software applications are usually either application-specific client software you will get from the supplier of the product, IP service applications such as Telnet (software that permits a PC to emulate a terminal while communicating with another computer over a network), or a Web browser. Products designed to work with a general Web browser may also require specific helper applications that extend the functionality of Web browsers. If so, note them on Workform K.

If the supplier of the product under consideration has indicated any other software requirements to support the product, note them on Workform K under Other Software. A vendor's graphical online catalog client might require a word processing program to create bibliographies for users, for example.

Part 2: Servers and Printers

Servers

Function

Servers are used for a wide variety of functions including collecting and sending e-mail, serving Web pages, sharing office applications, etc. Record the primary function of your server on Workform K.

Processor Type and Speed, RAM, Disk Space Needed, and Operating System

You will need to identify the same four technical requirements for servers that you did for PC clients: processor type and speed, RAM, disk space needed, and operating system.

CD Server

If the option under consideration includes CD-ROMs, you will also want to note the number of CD drives you will need to support the product and the drive speed recommended by the supplier. Speed indicates the rate at which data is transferred from the CD to the computer. It is described by a number followed by *X,* for example, 2X, 12X, 24X. The larger the number, the faster the speed.

Other Requirements

If there are other server requirements indicated by the supplier of the product under consideration, specific peripherals such as tape drives or floppy disk drives, for example, note them under Other Requirements on Workform K.

Printers

As you consider each product and service, give some thought to the output options you want to offer to your customers. Will they be likely to want to print information from the product? If so, do you intend to offer a printer with each workstation, or will you want to use networked printers that are shared by multiple workstations? Will you supply the paper and ink, or do you intend to charge for print services? Does the printer need to be a color printer?

If you intend to charge your patrons for printing, think about how you intend to collect the money. Some libraries operate on an honor system, asking patrons to pay after they print. Other libraries choose to locate the printer behind a public service desk, where the money is collected when the patron receives the printouts. Still others have installed coin- or card-operated printers that require the patron to pay before the printouts are produced. If you elect to place the printer behind a desk, it will need to be a networked printer. With the honor system, you can use either networked or individual workstation printers. With a coin- or card-operated system, you will need to investigate the requirements of the system you intend to use to determine whether it supports networked or individual printers.

Although networked printers might seem to be an obvious choice, there are some privacy concerns and issues about identifying the output that you should consider before you commit to networked printers. With individual printers, patrons can control who sees their output; the printer is typically located next to the PC and the patron can remove the printout immediately after the printing is done. Networked printers receive multiple print jobs from multiple PCs, and the print jobs are handled sequentially from a print queue. If five patrons send print jobs to the printer at the same time, the printing is done sequentially; each job is completed before the next one is begun. This means you could have patrons standing around the printer waiting for their pages to come off and perusing other people's print jobs as they print. If the printer is behind a public service desk, patrons have to ask for their information and will assume the staff has looked at it.

Many products lack a good way to label a printout as belonging to a particular user. In Windows 95 networks, for example, networked printouts can be produced with a cover sheet. However, the cover sheet includes only the network name of the PC that produced it, not the patron who was using the PC. This can lead to patrons sorting through multiple printouts searching for the information they printed. Some products have a way for the patron to input identification to include on a cover sheet. If the products you are considering don't have that feature, you will want to give serious thought to the public-service implications of shared printers before you choose network printing.

On Workform K on the Networked line, circle yes or no as appropriate and indicate the number of printers of each type you need.

Regardless of whether the printers are networked or connected to individual workstations, you will still need to identify the technical requirements for the printers you need, including whether they connect to the workstation or network printer server via a serial or a parallel connection, whether color printing is required or desirable, and what print resolution will best support the output from this product.

Part 3: Networks

Networks can be both local area networks (LANs) and wide area networks (WANs). A LAN connects computers in a workgroup, department, or building. LANs require data cabling that serves as the medium for the message passing between the devices. A WAN is a communications system that connects geographically dispersed computers or LANs, usually in two or more separate buildings. A WAN typically uses a telephone connection between sites to serve as the message-passing medium.

Before you can determine the network infrastructure requirements for each of your best-choice options, you need to answer several basic questions:

- Does this option require a PC to access an information product or software?
- Does this option require shared access to an information product or software?
- If so, where will that product or software be located?
- Does this option require shared access to certain hardware resources, such as printers or CD-ROM drives?
- If so, where will that hardware be located?
- How much data traffic will be generated by users of the shared resources?

If you need assistance with these questions, optional Workform L: Network Decision Tree may help you. If you answer "yes" to shared software, information products, or hardware resources, you will most likely need a local area network to accomplish your objectives. You may also need a server or other special hardware to provide access to the software or information product. If you identify more than one site that will be sharing the resources, or a resource that is not physically located in the same facility as the users, you will need a wide area network. If you have multiple facilities, you will probably need a LAN in each one and a WAN to connect them. Even if your remote sites have only a collection of PCs and a telephone connection to a central site, that collection of PCs and the hub(s) and data cabling that connect them to the communications equipment and the phone line are actually a complete LAN.

Local Area Network (LAN)

Once you have determined that you will need a LAN, you then need to decide what type of network you need and how fast it must be.

Type

The type of network is defined by two standards, a Media Access Control (MAC) standard and a data transmission standard. The two most common MAC standards are Ethernet and Token Ring. Most libraries use Ethernet; Token Ring is used in IBM networks. The two most common data transmission standards are TCP/IP and IPX/SPX. TCP/IP is the standard of the Internet, so most library vendors develop their products to work with TCP/IP. IPX/SPX is used in Novell networks. Although it is possible to mix both TCP/IP and IPX/SPX on the same Ethernet network, it is easier to manage a network with only one data transmission standard. (More information on these standards can be found in the Tech Note on Communications Protocols and TCP/IP Services.)

Speed

Network speed is defined by the number of bits of data that can be transmitted between devices per second. Standard Ethernet LANs can transmit 10 million bits per second (Mbps). To put this in perspective, consider the representative file sizes shown in figure 1.

If you are planning to share only character-based bibliographic data across your network, a 10 Mbps Ethernet LAN will probably meet your needs. Even if your network is operating at an average of 50 percent capacity (the recommended limit to ensure acceptable response time), you can comfortably transfer the equivalent of 625 MARC records a second.

However, if you are planning to add multimedia CD-ROMs to the network, you may find that 10 Mbps isn't enough. A 10-second thumbnail video clip in a CD-ROM encyclopedia can contain 6 million bits of data. Two users requesting video clips at the same time could overload the network. Fortunately, there is also a standard for Fast Ethernet, which permits devices to exchange data at 100 Mbps. A standard for Gigabit Ethernet, 100 times faster than Fast Ethernet, has just been adopted. Each of these speeds requires different network hardware, and Gigabit Ethernet may require different data cabling. Fast Ethernet and Gigabit Ethernet offer growth paths for library networks as more and more resources become electronic and need a network to be delivered.

FIGURE 1
File Size Comparison Chart

Type of File	Number of Bits
Circulation transaction	300
Typical OPAC display	2,400
Full MARC record	8,000
Thumbnail graphic	400,000
30-second sound file	1.8 million
Half-screen, high-quality photograph	2.4 million
3-minute video clip	200 million

Hubs and Terminal Servers

Once you have determined the type and speed of the LAN or LANs you will need, you need to identify the network equipment you will require to support the LAN. Network equipment for a LAN includes hubs and may include terminal servers as well. Information on network equipment can be found in Network Equipment Glossary in the Tech Notes.

Hubs, which connect networked devices to each other, can connect four to twenty-four or more devices. Large networks often include multiple hubs. Note the number of connections you need to support in the Description part of Workform K. Then determine how many hubs you will need for that number of connections.

Terminal servers are used to connect character-based terminals to a computer over a network. Like hubs, they include a number of ports, typically ranging from eight to sixteen. If the option you are considering can be supported with character-based terminals, you will most likely need terminal servers.

Hubs and terminal servers are available for both Ethernet and Token Ring networks. Be sure the information you gather is for equipment compatible with the type of network you intend to install. Hubs are capable of supporting either 10 or 100 Mbps network speeds. Some hubs can support either speed with the setting of a switch. Be sure to note the speed your option requires. Ether switches are special types of hubs that can support 10 and 100 Mbps speeds simultaneously.

Terminal servers also need to be compatible with the type and speed of your LAN. In addition, terminal servers need to support the protocol your product requires.

Wide Area Network (WAN)

If you are trying to connect users in one location with products or databases in another location, you will need a wide area network. A communications system between branch libraries and an automated circulation/online catalog system at the central library is an example of a WAN. A dedicated connection from a library to its Internet service provider is a form of WAN as well.

Internal and External WANs

Libraries that have an internal WAN, a communications system that links branches to a central site, often mix the requirements of a text-based local system with graphical Internet access over a single WAN connection to each branch. In this environment, planning for sufficient bandwidth is critical to patron satisfaction with the library's core services of circulation and catalog access. If the bandwidth is being used to deliver graphical data to Internet terminals, circulation transactions and online catalog requests will experience response time delays. (More information about bandwidth can be found in a following section and in the Tech Notes.)

Even libraries that don't need internal WANs often have external WANs. External WANs are connections between libraries and suppliers of network services, such as Internet Service Providers (ISPs). Libraries with internal WANs also typically have an external WAN connection to an ISP for the entire organization. Sometimes multifacility libraries with no need for an internal WAN will have individual external WAN connections in each facility. A dial-up account from a PC using a modem and a voice-grade telephone line is a form of an external WAN connection.

The bandwidth of an external WAN connection is as important as the bandwidth of internal connections. This is particularly true when a single external connection to an ISP is meant to serve the needs of multiple sites on the internal WAN. In that case, the bandwidth of the external WAN connection to the central site needs to be calculated for the demand that will be generated by all of the potential simultaneous users at all of the internal WAN sites.

You should be aware that Internet service providers usually charge on a sliding scale for their services. The more bandwidth you have in your connection to an ISP, the more costly that ISP's monthly service charge will be.

Communication Links

Although some WANs are built on wireless technologies or cable television systems, most of the WANs libraries use are based on telephone connections between sites. Sometimes these telephone connections are based on dial-up connections between modems, established over voice-grade phone lines; more often they are based on dedicated digital phone circuits used to connect two or more sites. Detailed information on WAN options can be found in the Telecommunications Options Tech Note.

WANs can be based on any of several different telephone company services, but not every phone company offers every service. You will need to talk with your local telephone company to determine which services are available in your area. If your library deals with several different phone companies because of the geographic distribution of your branches, you will need to determine which services are available from each company. Your choices of WAN equipment will be limited by the services available from your phone company.

Bandwidth

The amount of data transfer capacity a network has is called its bandwidth. Capacity planning for a network is a little like selling airline seats. Airline reservationists expect that not everyone who reserves a seat will actually travel on a flight; network designers expect that only some of the connected devices will be using the network at any one time. However, you need to understand the types and approximate sizes of the files that each of the applications on the network will be transferring and estimate the frequency with which those transfers will take place to plan a reasonable network bandwidth. Just as with the airline flights, sometimes your network will be "oversold"; that is, the active devices will be requesting more than the bandwidth can deliver. When this happens you will experience a slow response time. Everyone who has ever been on the Internet has had experience with slow response time; the same thing can happen in your own LAN or WAN. A reasonable objective in network bandwidth planning is to plan for the average load, leaving some excess capacity to handle most of the peaks of demand.

Bandwidth planning is part science and part art, based on simple mathematics and informed estimates. The science part is that each LAN or WAN connection has a fixed capacity available, and you have to work within those limits. The art part is estimating how many characters-per-second each device on your network is actually contributing to the overall use of the bandwidth because it is based on exactly what resources are being accessed at each device at any given moment in time. Obviously a circulation transaction that is based on passing a bar code number uses less of the bandwidth than the results of an OPAC search.

Most WAN services offer you the same bandwidth for both incoming and outgoing data. However, many of the data transfers done in libraries are not symmetrical. Data requests tend to be small, and data delivery is large. Think of a typical online catalog inquiry. At a subject prompt, a patron enters "dogs," and the response includes bibliographic information for thirty or forty titles. In other words, a four-character request generates thousands of characters of response. Internet searching is very asymmetrical as well. A single mouse click can request a 5,000-character Web page.

Internet access only complicates the picture. A growing number of Web sites include photographs or high-resolution graphics. The impression of motion on a Web page is often created by feeding small programs every couple of seconds to a client device. Each of these changing logos or advertisements also consumes bandwidth. Therefore, any rules of thumb used in network bandwidth planning are estimating tools, not immutable facts. Each site will be different, and each day or hour of the day will be different, too.

Although it is possible to engineer a WAN connection to ensure three- to five-second response time for applications under your control, such as circulation and OPAC applications, once you add the vagaries of the Internet to the picture you can only estimate your needs. On the Internet, response time is a function of your bandwidth, overall Internet usage that day, the size of the server you are connected with, and the number of other users on that server. The best you can do is to plan for a good average response time and understand that there will be times when the response time is beyond your control.

Telecommunications equipment manufacturers are beginning to develop software for their equipment that will support "reserving" bandwidth for particular types of data traffic. Because of the technical skills needed, most libraries will need to depend on their library automation system vendors to implement these features before they will be of benefit to libraries.

WAN connections have much less capacity than LANs. In fact, the capacity of a library's WAN will only be a fraction of the capacity of its LANs. The two most common speeds for WAN connections are 56 Kbps (referred to as 56K) and T1. It is also possible in some regions of the country to license a fraction or portion of a T1 line; these are referred to as FT1 lines. A 56K connection is capable of passing 56,000 bits of data per second between two sites. A T1 connection can pass 1.544 million bits per second. Compare those speeds with the LAN speeds given previously. It would take seven T1 WAN lines to equal the speed of a standard 10 Mbps Ethernet.

Some phone companies offer T3 lines (45 million bits per second), but the costs generally make these prohibitive for libraries. For a library that has exceeded the capacity of a single T1, adding another T1 is usually the most cost-effective next step. There are a number of other options for higher bandwidth under development, including Asynchronous Transfer Mode (ATM), public/private fiber utilities, even the Internet 2 initiative. Fortunately, libraries are not the only organizations with high bandwidth requirements, so commercial and business needs will drive the development of a multitude of higher bandwidth options. It is far from clear at this time which technologies will ultimately be commercially viable and how long the development will actually take.

Again, to give this some perspective, let's consider how long it would take to transfer files over 56K versus T1 WAN connections. As you read figure 2, remember that these speeds assume that only one file is being transferred. If

FIGURE 2
Transaction Speed Comparison Chart

Type of File	Number of Bits	Transfer Time at 56K Speed	Transfer Time at T1 Speed
Circulation transaction	300	.005 of a second	Too fast to calculate
Typical OPAC display	2,400	.04 of a second	Too fast to calculate
MARC record	8,000	.14 of a second	.005 of a second
Thumbnail graphic	400,000	7 seconds	1/3 of a second
30-second sound file	1.8 million	32 seconds	1.2 seconds
Half-screen, high-quality photograph	2.4 million	43 seconds	1.6 seconds
3-minute video clip	200 million	59.5 minutes	2 minutes 9 seconds

the WAN connection is actually being used by multiple devices, some number of which are sending or receiving data, then the actual transfer times will be slower than the figure indicates.

Clearly, if you are only using your WAN to transfer circulation transactions and online catalog records between facilities, the 56K speed is probably fast enough for your needs. Your staff can't scan a bar code every .005 of a second, nor are your patrons likely to request full MARC records seven times a second. In fact, most automated system vendors suggest that you can support twenty-five to forty text-based terminals or workstations on a 56K WAN connection with acceptable response time.

If you are delivering full-text periodical information from a centrally located database over that same 56K line, however, you will occasionally exceed the bandwidth. A single page of text can carry up to 2,000 characters of data, or 16,000 bits. These pages would transfer at three and a half pages per second over a 56K WAN connection, and while they were transferring no other data (for example, circulation transactions or OPAC results) would be passed.

If you are trying to deliver graphical Internet content over that 56K connection, two to five PCs surfing the Internet can tie up the entire capacity of the line. In the 1995 NCLIS study, *Internet Costs and Cost Models for Public Libraries,* McClure estimated that twenty-five graphical devices would require a T1 line for adequate response time, which is nearly 56K per device.[1] Of course, this assumes that all the devices are sending and receiving at the same time. Remember the airline parallel: not everyone who has a reservation takes the flight. In a network, every device is not actually sending or receiving data all the time. Much of the time the user is reading the screen and deciding what to ask for next; the user isn't taking up the network's capacity during that time, so the bandwidth is available to others.

Part 4: Staff Skills

If the option you are considering requires your staff to have specific technical skills to effectively use the product or service, you should identify those necessary skills in Part 4 of Workform K.

Put an *X* next to the level of each skill you estimate will be required. Then enter the current number of staff who will be using this product at each skill level. You only need to estimate the skills of the staff who will use the specific product you are considering. For example, if you are evaluating the requirements of a collection of business periodicals in electronic format, you only need to estimate the skills of your reference staff who will be working with that product. Let's assume you have eight people on your reference staff. If you think three of them have basic Windows skills and five of them have a high degree of comfort with Windows, your response for that section of Part 4 would look like that shown in figure 3.

FIGURE 3
Sample Staff Skills Estimate

Staff:_____	Level of Skill Needed	Current Skill Level of Staff Users	Number of Staff Needing Training
Windows skills			
None			
Basic	X	3	0
Expert		5	0

Part 5: Public Skills

If the option you are considering requires your users to have specific technical skills to effectively use the product or service, you should identify those necessary skills in Part 5 of Workform K. Use the estimates you developed in Workform F to determine what percentage of users might need training to effectively use the option under consideration. For example, if you think the product requires basic skill with a Web browser and you estimated on Workform F that 40 percent of your users had some browser skills and 20 percent had high-level browser skills, you would enter that information as shown in figure 4 .

Part 6: Technical Skills

If your plans include PCs or networks, you will need technical skills as well, either on staff or available to you through other sources. These skills include basic software loading, system configuration, and troubleshooting skills for both PCs and networks. Technical skills may be hired, developed on staff through training, or provided by an external agency, such as a city or county information services department, a local network support company, or your library automation vendor.

FIGURE 4
Sample Public Skills Estimate

	Level of Skill Needed	Percentage Estimate of Current Skill Level	Percentage of Public Needing Training
Web-browser skills			
None		40	40
Basic	X	40	0
Expert		20	0

Use Part 6 of Workform K to identify the specific skills that will be needed for the option you are studying and to identify the availability of those skills. If you expect to acquire some of the needed skills from outside the library, note where you expect those skills to come from in the last column of the form.

How Do You Use the Information on Workform K to Identify a Proposed Infrastructure?

Each of the three copies of Workform K you have completed identifies the hardware, software, networks, and skills you need to implement the product or service options under review. Now you need to compare those three sets of requirements.

Completing Workform M: Infrastructure Requirements Comparison

Use Workform M: Infrastructure Requirements Comparison to summarize the information you have gathered on Workform K for each of the three options under review. The object of this evaluation process is to identify the infrastructure investments that will support the largest number of your high-priority options. This will be the primary infrastructure in your technology plan. It will be the basis for delivering the product and service options you have already identified and will provide you with major criteria you will use in the evaluation of additional products.

Study the information on Workform M.

What are the points of commonality among the infrastructure requirements for the three product or service options?

Could you support all three with a single infrastructure investment?

Do all of the options require PCs and Internet access?

Will they require an internal WAN between your central library and your branches?

Circle "Yes" in the Proposed Infrastructure column for those components that appear in two or more activities. Write the information on the terminal protocol required and operating systems in that column as well.

Although it is unlikely, you may find that your three options do not have common infrastructure components. If so, you will need to repeat Task 9: Identify a Proposed Infrastructure for the next two or three options on your priorities list, add these activities to Workform M: Infrastructure Requirements Comparison, and look again for a dominant infrastructure.

It is also possible that some of your high-priority options will not be supported by the dominant infrastructure you have identified. In later tasks, you will have the opportunity to reassess these options and possibly determine additional infrastructure elements you may add to the technology plan. For now, let's focus on developing the proposed infrastructure and determining what would be required to implement that infrastructure.

Completing Workform N: Gap Analysis

Step One

Working with Workforms K: Infrastructure Evaluation and M: Infrastructure Requirements Comparison, you need to transfer information about the infrastructure you require to Workform N: Gap Analysis. For each "Yes" you have circled in the Proposed Infrastructure column of Workform M, you should enter the number of devices you will need on Workform N. This will be easier if you create a summary copy of Workform K for the devices you need in the proposed infrastructure.

Begin by making a clean copy of Workform K and label the Option line "Summary of Options." Study the three completed copies of Workform K, looking at the number of devices you determined you need for each option. For example, one option might be "licensing access to a Web-based business periodicals collection for each facility," and you may have determined on Workform K that you will require ten PCs for each facility. A second option might be to "provide homework help by licensing a CD-ROM product for each facility." Your completed Workform K indicates that you will need six PCs at each facility to support this option.

You need to determine if these two options can be served by the same PCs. Will the homework help PCs be installed in the same location as the business periodical PCs? Or do you intend to put the homework PCs in the children's area and the business PCs in the adult reference department? If the two options will be offered in the same physical space, you may need only ten PCs. If the homework help devices will be at separate locations at each facility where you plan to offer the service, then you will need sixteen PCs at each facility. Write the number you determine you need in the "Number Needed" box on a summary copy of Workform K.

Continue working through each device listed in Workform K. If the Workform M analysis shows you need a particular device, use the completed Workform Ks to help you determine how many of those devices you need. Enter the total number of devices you need on the summary copy of Workform K.

When you have completed the Number Needed column on the summary copy of Workform K, transfer this information to the Need box on Workform N: Gap Analysis. This will give you a set of requirements to use in the next task.

TASK 10
Determine What It Will Cost to Implement the Proposed Infrastructure

In this task you will compare your current environment with the proposed Infrastructure you developed on Workform M. By identifying the gaps between what you own now and what you need, you will develop a list of the software, hardware, networks, and training necessary to support your highest priority options. You will then develop cost estimates for the infrastructure components you need to purchase. When you have finished the task you will have determined the projected costs for each of the necessary investments.

Who is responsible for Task 10?

The planning committee chair will lead this task.

Who else is involved in Task 10?

The planning committee members will be involved.

What data is needed for Task 10?

The data needed is on Workforms F, G, M, N, O, and P.

What workforms are used in Task 10?

Workform F: Current Technology Overview
Workform G: Facility Review
Workform N: Gap Analysis
Workform O: Summary of Investments Needed for Proposed Infrastructure
Workform P: Summary of Purchase and Ongoing Costs

What outside assistance would be helpful in Task 10?

You might ask staff with technical expertise to help the committee members identify the projected costs for the needed infrastructure.

> *Enhanced level of effort:* You might hire an outside consultant to complete this task. The committee would then review and revise the consultant's recommendations as needed.

How long will Task 10 take?

The time-consuming part of this task is determining the cost information for Workform O: Summary of Investments Needed for Proposed Infrastructure. The time required will depend on the investments needed and the number of people involved in getting cost estimates. When they finish, the committee will spend one meeting completing Workform N: Gap Analysis. Workform O will be completed prior to the next meeting, which will begin with a review and discussion of Workform O.

How Do You Determine What You Will Need to Purchase for Your Proposed Infrastructure?

When you started this technology planning process, you began by assessing your current conditions on Workform F: Current Technology Overview. You may already have some of the elements of your proposed infrastructure in place. To determine the components you need to add, you will want to compare what you already have with the requirements of your proposed infrastructure. The difference, or "gap," is the hardware, software, networks, and training you will need to acquire before you can begin to do the activities in your service plan. You will also need to look again at Workform G: Facility Review. What potential problems, if any, did you discover with the readiness of your facility for new or additional technology? Until you close the gap between the proposed infrastructure and your current environment, you do not have the tools you need to proceed with your service plan.

Completing Workform N: Gap Analysis

Step Two

Use Workform N: Gap Analysis to compare the hardware, software, and networks you have today with the proposed infrastructure you developed in Task 9: Identify a Proposed Technology Infrastructure. Transfer the information from Workform F: Current Technology Overview to the Have columns of Workform N. In Task 9 you already transferred the information from the Proposed Infrastructure column of your summary of Workform K to the Need column on Workform N. Now compare the Have column with the Need column on Workform N to reveal the gap between the equipment your library already owns and the equipment you need when you offer the products and services you have selected. Record the differences between Have and Need in the Gap column. Then use the space for Plan for Filling Gap or Reallocating Surplus to indicate what it will take to close the gap between the existing equipment and the equipment needed for the proposed infrastructure or how you will reallocate any surplus.

For example, your proposed infrastructure may require five Pentium PCs with 32 MB of RAM running Windows 95. You may currently own five Pentium PCs with 8 MB of RAM running Windows 3.1. You will need to invest

FIGURE 5

Sample Gap Analysis

PCs	Have	Need	Gap
Processor type and speed: Pentium 133	5	5	0
RAM: 32 MB	8 MB each in 5 Pentiums	5 with 32 MB RAM	5 with 24 MB RAM upgrades
Hard drive space: 10 MB	5	5	0
Operating system: Windows 95	0	5	5
Color monitor (Y/N): Y	5	5	0
Speech synthesizer (Y/N): N	0	0	0
Adaptive keyboard (Y/N): N	0	0	0
Sound card (Y/N): N	0	0	0
Speakers or headphones (Y/N): N	0	0	0
Plan for filling gap or reallocating surplus			
Upgrade existing Pentiums to 32 MB of memory and purchase Windows 95 upgrades			

in at least 24 MB of RAM and Windows 95 for each PC to meet the infrastructure requirements. Another scenario is that you have 486 PCs, in which case you will need to either replace them with Pentiums or upgrade the 486 chip in your PCs to the Pentium chip, if that is technically possible. Figure 5 shows a sample gap analysis for PCs.

Completing Workform O: Summary of Investments Needed for Proposed Infrastructure

When you have completed Workform N, transfer the information from the Plan for Filling Gap or Reallocating Surplus section to Workform O: Summary of Investments Needed for Proposed Infrastructure. The following information may be helpful as you complete these two columns. Once you have identified what you need and how many are required, you will complete the Cost Per Unit and Total Cost columns of Workform O.

Part 1. Equipment Required

Workform O has separate lines to indicate the new client devices and servers you will need to add as well as upgrades you may want to consider for equipment you already own. Often an existing PC can be upgraded with more memory or disk storage at a lesser cost than purchasing a new machine. More comprehensive upgrades, such as replacing 486 chips with Pentium chips, are frequently just as expensive as purchasing new equipment, but you may want to investigate the options of upgrading prior to committing to purchasing new equipment. Workform O provides sections for recording the cost of purchasing new PCs or for recording the costs of upgrade components. (See the sections on costs that follow.)

Note, too, that the operating system information has been included in the PC section *and* in the Servers section of Workform O. New devices you buy will include the operating system, so as you begin to develop cost information for your plan, it makes sense to begin to group the operating system costs with the equipment costs.

Part 2. Software Required

Transfer to Part 2 of Workform O the information on the software you need to add. Remember that you can install free Internet helper applications such as the Adobe Acrobat reader or Real Audio on as many PCs as you need to at no additional cost, but you are required to purchase a copy of commercial software for each PC you have. Occasionally you will be able to purchase a site license for commercial software that will permit you to use an unlimited number of copies at a single site.

Part 3. Networks Required

Record the devices you need to support the networks you will install. Include here the communications links you must license from the phone company. The building wiring you need will be recorded in Part 7 of this form.

Part 4. Staff Skills

Workform O includes a place for you to estimate the costs of training staff in the skills you determined were needed but not yet available. These skills are as crucial to the success of your technology plan as any hardware or software you will buy. If your staff is not comfortable using the products you select, they will not use the investment to its fullest.

Part 5. Public Skills

There will be an expense associated with training the public to use products or services if they don't already have the needed technical skills. This is the hardest cost to estimate. You have already developed estimates of the percentage of the public that has certain technical skills. You might begin estimating the cost of training by applying that percentage to the number of patrons you serve on an average day. How many people will you work with who will need some basic training? How long will that training take?

Remember that all training is not equal. The time (and therefore, cost) required for training will be determined by the way you decide to deliver the training. For example, let us assume that you serve 600 users a week and you estimate 30 percent of them do not have the Web skills they will need to use the infrastructure you have selected. That means your staff will be working with up to 180 people a week who may need help getting the information they need. You could provide this help by having reference staff do 180 individual 10-minute sessions for a total of 1,800 minutes (30 hours) of staff time. On the other hand, you could schedule 1 hour of group training for up to 30 people 6 times a week, at a staff cost of 6 hours to present the training and maybe 4 hours to plan the training. Obviously, the second option requires less staff time. That does not automatically mean that it is the right choice for your library, but it is certainly an important factor to consider. Think about how you will address the need for public training, and estimate the hours of staff time you will need to invest.

Part 6. Technical Skills

If you intend to train your own staff in these skills, be sure to include the cost of any commercial training you will fund as well as the cost of staff members' time who will take the training.

If you intend to get these skills from outside suppliers, such as your city or county data processing staff or your library automation vendor, note the costs you will incur in the Total Cost Per Person column.

Part 7. Facility Upgrades

Finally, look again at Workform G: Facility Review. Did you identify problems there that will have to be addressed before you can implement your proposed infrastructure? Note those problems in the appropriate spaces on Workform O.

How Do You Estimate the Costs?

When you have completed the first two blank columns of Workform O, you will have a list of the investments you need to make to build your proposed infrastructure. These investments may include purchasing new hardware, installing LANs, or contracting for Internet services and/or different telephone lines between your facilities. You may also need to invest in training for some or all of your staff, and you may need to hire or train a technical manager or find a vendor that will take care of your technical management requirements. You may need to upgrade your electrical plant or purchase new furniture. What is this all going to cost? Can you afford it?

The infrastructure components you have determined that you need—hardware, software, and network equipment—can be purchased from a variety of sources. However, pricing for these components will range from the manufacturer's suggested retail price offered by full-service vendors to deeply discounted prices offered by mail order, Web sources, or technology super-stores. If you found some pricing information when you were researching your options to complete Workform K, those prices were probably the man-ufacturer's suggested retail prices. It is possible that you may be able to find a better price depending on your needs.

The purchase options for technology are very similar to shopping in depart-ment stores. If you want a personal shopper to help you pick out the perfect item, you go to Macy's, Dillard's, or Nordstrom and expect to pay retail prices. The store will arrange to have the item tailored, if need be, and may take a re-turn if you bring the item and sales slip back a month later. If you know what you want, don't mind waiting in line, and are willing to have it altered your-self, there are plenty of other stores that will sell you the same products at reduced prices. Just remember, you are expected to serve yourself—personal attention doesn't come with the reduced prices. This same spectrum ranging from full-service/retail pricing to self-service/discount pricing exists in the world of technology.

Full-Service Suppliers

Full-service suppliers will analyze your functional requirements and present you with a proposal for the hardware, software, training, installation, and maintenance of a range of technology products. They will take a request such as "We want to offer access to CD-ROMs from fifteen PCs in three sites" and design local area networks at each site linked by wide area connections. These suppliers will give you proposals that will suggest the server and client PC configurations you will need, including operating systems, and special CD management software; they may suggest menuing and license-monitoring software. Their services will even include providing you with site preparation information on the data cabling and electrical service you will need to support the network. Although you will need to know enough about the technology you are trying to install to be able to understand the components of the ven-dor's proposal, or at least enough to ask intelligent questions and understand the answers, working with a full-service supplier lets you "outsource" the de-sign of the infrastructure, the identification of an appropriate set of compo-nents, and the installation and testing of the products.

Full-service suppliers include many of the traditional library automation vendors and local or national network design firms. The advantage of using the traditional library vendors as full-service suppliers is their knowledge of the operational environment of public libraries. They usually understand that much of the technology on which they are being asked to quote will be used by the general public and that security of the client devices and ease of use are para-mount. (You will find more information on the pros and cons of purchasing everything from a single library automation vendor later in this chapter.)

Generalist network designers are more experienced with business applications and more oriented toward designing solutions to be used only by staff. Their assumptions about security needs revolve around keeping users from accessing specific network resources, not keeping them from accessing the client machine's operating system. A library that wants to work with a local networking firm that has had little or no public access experience needs to be very explicit about the operating environment. Sometimes a library consultant can help facilitate communication between the library staff and a local supplier that doesn't understand the library's environment.

Self-Service Suppliers

If you have the technical expertise on staff to design your own networks or to identify the components you want to buy to accomplish your objectives, you can create a list of the desired equipment and services and solicit price quotes from various potential suppliers. The degree of support you require in the installation, configuration, and testing of the equipment and software will determine which firms will give you quotes. Be sure to think through carefully the services you will need and be very explicit about them in whatever documents you produce to solicit quotes, whether those documents are simply letters requesting prices or more formal bid packages such as a Request for Proposal.

Underestimate rather than overestimate your staff's abilities to install and configure new equipment. Staff time costs money, too. If your staff has experience with the technology you are buying, for example, if you are adding fifteen PCs to an existing network of thirty-five PCs, then you may already know approximately how long it will take staff to install, test, and configure the new machines. You can compare the cost of doing the work in-house with the cost quotes for those services from your potential suppliers and decide which option makes the best financial sense. However, if the project represents a new challenge for your staff, you need to allow for the learning-curve costs. Often, it is best to hire the supplier to install the first phase of your new project and ensure that your staff members work with the supplier to learn what is being done. Then, in subsequent phases, you will have the expertise available on your staff to do the work in-house, if you choose.

Telecommunications Suppliers

The costs of the various phone services vary from state to state. The rates for telephone service are set by each state's public utility oversight agency; there is no standard for which service might be the most cost effective for a library to use. Each type of service requires a different set of communications hardware to operate your WAN. To identify the most cost-effective service, you need to consider three factors: installation costs, monthly service costs, and the cost of the necessary WAN hardware and software.

Most of the services are billed at a flat monthly rate per phone line. For some of the services, the monthly costs are "metered" costs. This means you pay for the time you spend connected. Sometimes the costs are based on a per-minute-connected rate, other times they are based on the number of calls you place. Be sure you understand the metering system if you are considering a metered service. For cost comparison purposes, if you don't know how long you expect to be connected, plan on being connected all of the hours the library is staffed. Remember, in some respects metered service punishes success. If you offer a service over a metered line and the service is very successful, the connection time will go up and so will the costs. If you start a service with a metered line, be sure your contract with the telephone company includes an option to switch to flat-rate service later, without a penalty. Then monitor your monthly costs and compare them with the costs for a flat-rate service. At some point, it may be less expensive to switch.

Most WAN services offer you the same data transfer rates for both incoming and outgoing data. As was mentioned earlier, many of the data transfers done in libraries are not symmetrical. Data requests tend to be small, and data delivery is large. Many of the regional phone companies are developing Asymmetrical Digital Subscriber Line (ADSL) services that will provide increased download capacity. ADSL is a phone technology that may be very useful for libraries when it is introduced.

Because telecommunications technology is changing so rapidly and service costs are in such flux, it is generally a good idea to commit to no more than a three-year contract for data telecommunications services. Even with a three-year contract, every library should review its telecommunications costs and available options at least once a year. Sometimes the cost benefits of switching to a new phone service outweigh the penalties of canceling a contract and the hardware infrastructure investment needed to add the new service.

What Costs Do You Need to Include in the Plan?

Use Workform P: Summary of Purchase and Ongoing Costs to record the initial and annual costs of the proposed infrastructure. You will first record the purchase cost. However, the costs of the options under consideration include more than just the original purchase price of the equipment and software. Those costs are only the tip of the "cost iceberg." The Gartner Group, a consulting firm that publishes studies on the total cost of ownership of PCs and other technologies, notes that the purchase price of PCs represents approximately 20 percent of the total cost of owning PCs over three years.[2] Installation, maintenance, training, and support make up the remaining 80 percent. The cost estimates for your technology plan need to include annual budgeting for support costs as well as estimates of the initial purchase costs.

Installation

For Parts 1 through 3 of Workform P: Summary of Purchase and Ongoing Costs, include the costs of installation even if you intend to do the installation and testing of your equipment and software with in-house staff. By planning for the costs of these activities, you can assess whether additional resources must be allocated. If you estimate the costs of having your staff install the products, you will also have a basis for comparing those costs with the proposed installation costs of your supplier. Depending on the complexity of the project, it might be less expensive to let the vendor do it, even if your staff has the skills.

Library staff members already have full-time responsibilities; if you plan to add the responsibility for significant technology installations to a staff member's job, you may need to temporarily transfer some of that person's usual responsibilities to another staff member or to temporary employees. If that same person will be responsible for the ongoing maintenance of the new technologies, some of the job responsibilities that were temporarily transferred may need to become permanent transfers.

Annual Costs

Annual Costs to be calculated for Parts 1 through 3 of Workform P include maintenance, amortization, and support costs.

Maintenance

Include the costs for any maintenance contracts you have on the equipment you purchase. Even if you elect to repair equipment on an as-needed, time-and-materials basis, you still should budget an amount each year to pay for needed repairs. If you have a history with the type of equipment you are purchasing, use that history to estimate annual repair allowance per piece of equipment. If you are purchasing a new type of equipment and have no history to base estimates on, get an estimate from your repair source for the average cost of a repair, and plan on at least one repair expense per year for each piece of equipment. You can adjust your budget in subsequent years based on actual experience. Remember that older equipment usually fails more frequently and is more expensive to repair.

Amortization Allowance

Like many of the books on your shelves, your hardware and software will become "dated" and will need to be weeded. This will happen because new or upgraded software requires more processing power or memory than your current equipment can support or because the equipment you have is becoming increasingly expensive to maintain. Many public agencies amortize the replacement costs of technology over five years. This means they set aside 20 percent of the purchase price of the hardware and software each year for five years in a fund that will be used to replace the equipment at the end of the amortization period. Businesses often use three years for their amortization because of the pace of technological development. Use three if you can, five if you must, but include in your budgeting process an annual allowance for replacing the critical technologies your library users depend on. If you spend $10,000 on PCs in one fiscal year, three to five years later you will need another $10,000 to upgrade or replace that equipment. Technology is an ongoing operational expense, just as your materials budget is, and you need to explicitly recognize that in your technology plan.

Support

Support costs include estimates of the amount of time staff will spend loading new software updates and troubleshooting problems. If you have six PCs with filtering software that will require a monthly installation of updated software, and that software installation requires one hour per PC, allocate the costs of seventy-two staff hours (six hours in each of twelve months) per year for support. The amount of time you will need to allow for troubleshooting PC, printer, network, and server problems is a function of how well-trained your operating staff is and how much technical expertise your support staff has. The better trained your staff is, the fewer the problems that will develop.

Again, if you have information on your current support costs, use that to project the costs of supporting the new infrastructure. If you have no history to base your projections on, the following rules of thumb in the technical support industry may help you develop projections until you develop your own data.

In the typical office automation environment, each PC is customized to the requirements of its user. Each user selects his or her own software packages and maintains his or her own files as well as sharing files. It is estimated that PC support in this office environment requires one full-time equivalent (FTE) person for every fifty PCs. If you control the environment, specifying a common set of PC components and insisting that all the installed software be the same version of a limited set of programs and be configured the same across all machines, these support estimates can change to one FTE for every 100 to 125 machines.

Some simple operational actions will help control the costs of maintaining PCs as well. Remember that in an office environment each personal computer usually has a primary user, someone for whom a functioning keyboard and mouse, paper in the printer, and a clean monitor screen are important. This "owner" can be expected to stay abreast of the housekeeping details of operating a PC. By contrast, in a library, where half or more of the end-user devices are public access devices, a member of the public will typically move to another available device if the one he or she first approaches has an operational problem. Problems are usually only reported during high-use periods, when staff time to fix a problem is at a premium. It therefore falls to the library staff to monitor and maintain the devices as a part of their daily routine. Libraries need "technology pages" to monitor the PCs just as they need book pages to return the materials to the shelves. All too often, these simple, time-consuming tasks fall on highly trained reference librarians who spend their time working with equipment rather than with patrons. Depending on the number of public access devices you are intending to install, you may want to include some additional hours in the budget for staff time spent monitoring the equipment.

Should You Buy Everything from Your Library Automation System Vendor?

As electronic information products and technology-based library services increase, more vendors enter the field of library automation, each specializing in a particular niche of the marketplace, such as local systems vendors, CD-ROM networking specialists, electronic content producers, and personal computer vendors. The library automation industry was founded originally on the concept of "turnkey vendors." Systems were developed and sold on the basis of needing no technical expertise to operate. Vendors accepted full responsibility for the installation, testing, performance, and service of their systems, giving the libraries a single point of contact for any hardware or software problems.

The turnkey approach worked effectively for most libraries in the 1970s and 1980s, and it continues to work for some libraries today. However, for most libraries, classic library automation—that which automates MARC database development and management, circulation control, serials and acquisitions, and provides an online public access catalog—is no longer enough. CD-ROM towers, World Wide Web servers, Internet-based electronic resources, local area networks, office automation, connection to city or county "enterprise wide" local/wide area networks, and connection to statewide networks of licensed electronic resources are all elements of modern libraries. Most traditional library automation vendors have been reluctant, or at least slow, to add support for these functions to their product lines. As a result, many libraries are grappling now with the issues of managing multiple vendors and products and accepting a much higher level of responsibility for integrating multiple systems than has ever before been necessary.

There can be advantages for a library with little or no technical expertise to try to maintain a turnkey relationship with the primary supplier of its technology. The vendor can provide much of the troubleshooting and management of the various infrastructure components in place. However, there can be disadvantages as well. You are at the mercy of your vendor with regard to network design, equipment selection, and network management. You are limited to selecting from among only those products your vendor is willing to provide, not the products that best meet your needs or are most cost effective. If your local phone company offers a new telecommunications option that could reduce your monthly costs but your vendor hasn't included equipment to support that option in its product line, you can't take advantage of it. Even if the vendor is willing to procure and install the new equipment for you, although it isn't a part of the main product line, you will always have trouble getting service and support because you will be the only such installation on the vendor's customer list.

The emergence of niche library vendors and the adoption of technologies developed outside the library marketplace are proving to be dual-edged swords. Libraries benefit from the focused expertise of specialists who develop hardware and software solutions to specific information delivery problems, such as serving the access needs of multiple simultaneous CD-ROM users or developing user-friendly graphical interfaces to complex text-oriented files. However, you may find the options you have chosen cannot be supported by products available from your automation vendor. If that is the case, you will need to look elsewhere for the products and services you require.

If You Don't Buy from Your Library Automation System Vendor, Where Can You Get Help if You Need It?

If your library doesn't have the technical expertise on staff to manage a network or the integration of multiple vendors' products, you can use several strategies to control the impact of a multivendor environment. These include selecting products with the same infrastructure requirements, which limits the number of technologies you need to master; implementing new technologies one at a time, with a phased roll-out plan so that you can test products and train staff to support them in a controlled environment; and, when possible, using off-site products, such as electronic resources mounted on the Internet, rather than products that need to be loaded and maintained locally.

Another alternative is to hire a local technology-support contractor or to use the city or county's information services department to do your implementations and network expansion tasks for you. While a local supplier won't initially bring you the library expertise a library vendor would, a supplier who is interested in your business will begin to develop some familiarity and experience with your unique environment and can develop into a valuable partner. Library staff will still need to be involved in specifying what needs to be done and monitoring the project plan to ensure that the implementation of new products doesn't unduly affect the library's ongoing operations. Staff will also need to be involved in testing the contractor's work to ensure that the project has been satisfactorily completed, but that testing can be done from the perspective of the end-user: Can you access the product at all the work-stations you expected to? Is the response time acceptable? Can you use the product from off-site? Can you get into the operating system and make changes you shouldn't be able to make?

Tie the final payments you make to successful testing of the contractor's work, especially if you don't intend to use the contractor's services for ongoing maintenance of the equipment. Be sure that the contractor leaves you with documentation on the project, too. Before you make the final payment, you should have a list of the equipment and software installed and a "map" of the network that identifies each piece of network equipment by its network address and details the connections between the equipment. You should have copies of the manufacturer's manuals for both hardware and software and a complete set of the software in a medium you can use to reload if it becomes necessary. Make these expectations clear in your contract for services, and don't complete your payments until they have been met.

Can Outsourcing Help?

A library can benefit in a number of ways from outsourcing elements of its technology planning and implementation. Hiring a consultant to help with developing your technology plan will reduce the time it takes to identify options, gather cost data, analyze the infrastructure requirements, and develop an implementation plan. Using a vendor to design and install a network will relieve you of the need to hire staff with network implementation skills. Contracting with a local PC support firm to maintain and troubleshoot your PCs and servers will allow your staff time to focus on delivering library services instead of being used as computer mechanics. About the only thing outsourcing probably won't do is save you large amounts of money.

Outsourcing can be a money saver when it is used to displace costs you are already incurring. For example, if you are paying three people to index the local newspaper and you can hire a commercial company to do the same work for less than the salaries of those three staff members, you save money if you stop paying those three staff members. More commonly, libraries reallocate those staff members to meeting a different organizational need, which means the overall out-of-pocket expenses increase, but the costs of meeting the new need are mitigated by the hours freed from the indexing project.

Most of the technology-related activities that libraries seek to outsource are not jobs that are already being done by staff; most are new requirements that the library needs to add to its list of necessary tasks. This means there are few existing costs to displace. The cost benefits of outsourcing technology-related functions are in the relative cost benefits of hiring specialists as needed versus the costs of employing and deploying your own staff to achieve the same results. For example, it may take a library staff member eight hours to install and configure a PC; a local PC installer could do the same work in two hours. With library staff then devoting a half an hour to testing the installer's work, even if the installer's charges per hour are twice that of the staff members' hourly wages, the library still "saves" money by using the installer.

A number of outsourcing opportunities are available to libraries. Among these are

> using a vendor to design, install, and maintain local area networks
>
> hiring an electrician or building contractor to install LAN wiring (not only highly recommended, but usually required by local building codes)
>
> leasing PCs and servers rather than purchasing them
>
> contracting with a local firm or city or county department to troubleshoot and support PCs, including loading and periodically updating software
>
> sending staff to local community colleges or computer store classes for basic PC skills and network management training
>
> buying self-paced video and software training programs to train staff to use commercial software packages such as word processing and spreadsheets or buying similar programs from library automation vendors for specialized library applications when available
>
> contracting with third-party application support "help desks" to provide assistance with commercial software packages such as word processing and spreadsheets (Commercial help desks are too expensive for most libraries, but if you are a part of a larger city or county organization, or a regional library system, you may be able to participate in a contract for such services.)
>
> contracting with a library automation system vendor to operate and manage your library system for you
>
> using a Web page developer to build and maintain the library's Web pages
>
> contracting with your ISP, city or county government, or a regional library to host your Web pages or manage your electronic mail

Other outsourcing choices are developing every day. Look into the options as you develop your cost estimates for installing, maintaining, and supporting the proposed infrastructure. Be prepared to review the options again as you get to the point of actually implementing your choices.

TASK 11
Obtain Preliminary Approval for the Proposed Infrastructure

In this task you will present your proposed infrastructure to the library director or library board for review and preliminary approval.

Who is responsible for Task 11?

The planning committee chair will be responsible for this task.

Who else is involved in Task 11?

The library director or the library board will review and act on the committee's recommendations. One or more committee members may assist the chair in presenting the recommendations to the library director or board. Alternatively, the library director may be asked to meet with the entire planning committee to review and discuss the recommendations.

What data is needed for Task 11?

Information about the proposed infrastructure and the costs associated with it provide the needed data. This information can be found on Workforms M and P.

What workforms are used in Task 11?

Workform M: Infrastructure Requirements Comparison
Workform P: Summary of Purchase and Ongoing Costs

What outside assistance would be helpful in Task 11?

None

> *Enhanced level of effort:* If an outside consultant was involved in determining your infrastructure requirements or the costs of the proposed infrastructure, you may wish to have the consultant present when making your recommendations.

How long will Task 11 take?

This can be accomplished in a single meeting.

Why Are You Requesting Approval before You Have Completed the Planning Process?

You have reached the point in this process where you will be making decisions that will affect the remainder of the process. There is not much point in selecting products and services that use your proposed infrastructure until that infrastructure has been reviewed and has received preliminary approval.

What Are You Presenting for Approval?

The library director and senior staff were involved in determining the priority of the activities in Task 5: Determine Which Activities Require Technology-Based Solutions. It is possible that was the last time they were actively included in the technology planning process. Therefore, you will want to present enough information to the people who will be reviewing your recommendations so they understand how you reached those recommendations. The extent of the background information required will vary depending on the people involved. Some directors will just want to look at the recommendations; others will want to be walked through every step of the process.

It would probably be helpful to use the completed Workform M: Infrastructure Requirements Comparison as the basis for your presentation. That workform includes the activities the director and senior staff selected as their highest priorities and the infrastructure requirements for each. You will probably also want to present Workform P: Summary of Purchase and Ongoing Costs. These two workforms should provide enough information for the director or board to give preliminary approval to your infrastructure selection. The director or board will probably want to review the entire plan after you have selected the products and services that will use your proposed infrastructure before giving final approval. You will also want to disseminate copies of the approved infrastructure with a short description of how it was developed to all staff members because they will be working with the infrastructure and will be interested in the decisions you are making.

What Do You Do if You Absolutely Cannot Afford Your Desired Infrastructure?

When you present Workform P to the library director or the library board for review and approval, the reality of your library funding picture comes into play. It may be that the library does not have the resources needed to implement the proposed infrastructure. In that case, the library director and the committee have several choices open to them.

First, they can look for cost savings inherent in the proposed infrastructure. If, for example, the proposed infrastructure includes a LAN, will that LAN allow you to purchase some reference materials on CD-ROM rather than in print form? If your proposed infrastructure includes Internet access, what impact will that have on your print reference collection? You may need to complete Task 12: Select the Products and Services That Use the Approved Infrastructure before you can determine these costs, but such potential savings are worth considering at this point. The director or board may decide to ask for more information before making any decision on the proposed infrastructure.

Another choice would be to raise some or all of the money required for initial installation of the infrastructure from outside sources, understanding that the library will still have to pay for the ongoing costs of the infrastructure. For more information on this choice see Task 14: Develop a Plan for Obtaining the Needed Resources.

A third choice would be to look at the costs of phasing in the installation of the infrastructure. For more information on this choice see Task 15: Develop an Implementation Time Line.

If none of these choices seems likely to result in the resources required to implement the proposed infrastructure, you may have to go back to Workform M: Infrastructure Requirements Comparison and identify a less expensive infrastructure that will accomplish at least some of your highest priority activities.

TASK 12
Select the Products and Services That Use the Approved Infrastructure

In this task you will review all of your product and service options to determine which can be used with the approved infrastructure. You will then select from among those the products and services that help you achieve your highest priority activities.

Who is responsible for Task 12?
The planning committee chair will lead this task.

Who else is involved in Task 12?
The planning committee members wil' select the activities and services.

What data is needed for Task 12?

The information about the approved infrastructure and the information gathered in Chapter 3: Discovering Your Options on available products and services and recorded on Workform I are needed.

What workforms are used in Task 12?

Workform I: Product/Service Options
Workform Q: Selected Products/Services

What outside assistance would be helpful in Task 12?

It would be very helpful to involve in the review process representatives from the people who will be using these products. You might want to appoint several subcommittees, each of which will review the options for a specific set of activities. Be sure to include at least one committee member on each subcommittee.

How long will Task 12 take?

The identification of possible products and services may take several weeks. The committee can select from among the options during one meeting.

What Criteria Do You Use to Select Technology-Based Products and Services?

At this point in your planning process you have defined the technical infrastructure that will provide the delivery mechanism for your information products and services. The hardware, operating systems software, and networks you plan to support are now known. This gives you the technical information you need to complete your evaluation of specific products and services, both for the highest priority activities with which you have been working and for the other activities for which you completed copies of Workform I: Product/ Service Options. Now that you have identified your infrastructure, you can be more focused on your search for options to support your activities. You can concentrate on products and services that will use the infrastructure you have selected. This will result in fewer options for each activity and will reduce the data gathering you need to do.

Go back to your copies of Workform I and first sort them by infrastructure requirements and then by activity. Separate the products and services that can be offered using your selected infrastructure. It is from these products and services that you will be making your first choices.

The first thing you will want to do is be sure that you have identified all of the possible vendors for your desired products or services. This may require additional research. Complete a copy of Workform I for each new product being reviewed. Once you have done that, you will look at the traditional library selection values of content, scope, authority, and frequency of updates as well as costs to determine your selection (much as you do with your print collection). You may want to involve your library's materials selection staff at this point to help select from among the options you have identified as using the proposed infrastructure.

Let's return to our example of providing access to business periodicals for the customers of the Anytown Library. If you have decided that your proposed infrastructure will include high bandwidth (T1 or FT1) access to the Internet from public access PCs in your main library and branches, then the option of accessing periodicals from a remote Internet site is supported by that infrastructure. However, there are many providers of business periodicals over the Internet. How do you choose one?

Most vendors will let you test the products, and it may be helpful to actually try each of the products. In the case of our business periodicals example, you might want to search each of the products for the same information and evaluate the number of hits you get. You may also want to do the same search several times in each product to see if the responses you get are consistent. This will help you determine the scope, authority, and quality of the indexing and retrieval features. You will also need to refine the cost information for each of the products you are reviewing and make a professional judgment on the value of each option relative to its price, just as you do with print materials.

When you have selected the product(s) and/or service(s) you intend to recommend to support one of your activities, use Workform Q: Selected Products/Services to record your choice.

How Do You Determine the Cost of a Product?

There are a number of ways to determine the cost of a product or service. You can get quotes for the cost of the product under consideration from its developer and often from "aggregators" or suppliers who make access to a number of electronic resources available from a single Internet site. OCLC's FirstSearch, DRA's DRANET, and Ameritech Library Services' Vista are some examples of commercially aggregated services. Many states are developing their own aggregation of electronic resources for public libraries in the state; Maryland's SAILOR and Ohio's OPLIN are two examples. Often the pricing for the same product from each of the sources can be quite different. Costs may also vary by the number of simultaneous users you want to support. Many vendors offer price breaks as the number of simultaneous users rises.

Some of the products you are considering may be products for which you know there is already a public demand. For example, you may be converting from print holdings of a selection of periodicals to electronic holdings. Because the public already knows about and uses these materials, you expect the broader distribution possibilities offered by electronic access will only increase the usage. Estimate the number of simultaneous users you expect to use your electronic holdings and use that as the basis of your cost projections. Ask, too, about the costs of adding users. Can it be done in one-user increments, or does the vendor license users in blocks of five or ten licenses? (See Task 7: Become Familiar with Current Technologies and Developing Trends for more information on licensing restrictions.)

Other products under consideration may need to be marketed to your target audience before they become heavily used. This would be true, for example, if you were planning to introduce a new service you had not previously supported. In this situation, it might make sense to try out a product on a pay-per-use basis if such an option is available. A set of databases might be available for an annual license fee of $3,000 per user from the developer or from an aggregator at $1 per use. If you project that use will grow as the service becomes known, it might make sense to get a license for X uses from the aggregator initially and plan to switch to an annual fee per simultaneous user as demand grows.

The same principle applies to services as well. If you intend to offer dial-in access to your online catalog for the first time, it may take time for the public to discover the service and begin to use it regularly. With each additional information resource you add, the time spent online in a dial-up connection will increase, and the demand will grow. As it does, you can add to the service by installing more modems and phone lines. If you intend to start small and "grow" the service, your cost estimates should include estimates of the next steps for expanding the service.

You may have gathered some of this cost information when you completed Workform I: Product/Service Options, but you will probably want to check those preliminary figures again. Prices change rapidly in the technology field.

TASK 13
Group the Remaining Activities and Begin Again at Task 8

Who is responsible for Task 13?

The planning committee chair will lead this task.

Who else is involved in Task 13?

The planning committee will complete this activity.

What data is needed for Task 13?

Refer to recommendations in Tasks 8 through 12.

What workforms are used in Task 13?

Workform I: Product/Service Options
Workform N: Gap Analysis

What outside assistance would be helpful in Task 13?

Refer to recommendations in Tasks 8 through 12.

How long will Task 13 take?

The length of time depends on how many of your activities could not be accomplished using your proposed infrastructure.

What Do You Do about the Activities That Cannot Be Accomplished Using Your Proposed Infrastructure?

You have now completed your first pass through the technology-related activities in your library's service plan. You have identified the infrastructure that supports your highest priority activities and selected the products and services that best meet your service goals, using that infrastructure. You have maximized the use of that infrastructure by selecting options that will use it for the remaining activities. However, you still may have activities for which you have completed copies of Workform I: Product/Service Options that can't be accomplished with your approved infrastructure. This may be because the products that support these activities are not available in a format compatible with your infrastructure. It may be the products are available but are more expensive than products available in a different format that meets your needs just as well or better. It may also be because the products for those options require a greater network bandwidth than your approved infrastructure offers.

If, for whatever reason, you find yourself with activities that require technology-based solutions that cannot be achieved using the infrastructure you have selected, you may decide that you want to include additional elements in your infrastructure. For example, you might add a CD-ROM server to the LAN you use with your Internet connection. If you have the resources to add to your infrastructure, you will select those elements in exactly the same way you selected your primary infrastructure.

To do this, start with the activities that cannot be accomplished with the first infrastructure. Using those activities, you will go back to Task 8: Evaluate the Options for Your Highest Priority Activities and go through the process again. This will help you identify a second set of infrastructure investments. When you do the gap analysis in Task 10, use the proposed infrastructure from the first pass in the "existing" column of Workform N: Gap Analysis.

When you complete this process you will have identified additional infrastructure requirements, determined their costs, received preliminary approval to include them in your plan, and selected the products and services that will be supported by this expanded infrastructure.

NOTES

1. Charles McClure, John Carlo Bertot, and John C. Beachboard, *Internet Costs and Cost Models for Public Libraries: Final Report.* (Washington, D.C.: U.S. National Commission on Libraries and Information Science, 1995): 14.

2. D. Cappuccio, B. Keyworth, and W. Kirwin, *Total Cost of Ownership: The Impact of System Management Tools* (Stamford, Conn.: The Gartner Group, 1996).

Chapter 5

Developing and Managing the Implementation Process

MILESTONES

By the time you complete this chapter you should

- know where you might obtain the resources you need to implement your plan

- understand what kind of purchases should be funded with grant funds

- understand the importance of monitoring the implementation of your technology plan

- understand the issues involved in phasing in the implementation of your plan

Making It Work

By the time you reach this point, you have expended a considerable amount of energy on deciding the technology infrastructure investments you need to make and selecting the products/services you intend to purchase. However, all of the decisions you have made still need to be implemented. This is a critical point in the process. You may have been involved in planning projects in the past that resulted in very nicely written plans that were read and discussed—and then filed on a shelf somewhere with similar plans. To ensure that all your hard work is going to lead to actual results, you will want to decide how your plan will be implemented and develop a process for monitoring that implementation.

These are the issues that will be addressed in the fifth planning step: Developing and Managing the Implementation Process. The three planning tasks you need to complete to accomplish this step are

TASK 14
Develop a Plan for Obtaining the Needed Resources

TASK 15
Develop an Implementation Time Line

TASK 16
Monitor Implementation and Make Adjustments as Needed

TASK 14
Develop a Plan for Obtaining the Needed Resources

In this task you will consider the various options for obtaining the resources required to implement your technology plan and develop a plan for obtaining those resources.

Who is responsible for Task 14?

The planning committee chair or the library director will take the lead in this task.

Who else is involved in Task 14?

The planning committee and the library director (if not taking the lead) will be involved. Other staff with fund-raising expertise, one or more board members, and a representative from the library Friends may also be involved in this task.

What data is needed for Task 14?

You will need to know what resources you require to implement your plan. You will also need to know how your local budget process works and understand how to write effective grants.

What workforms are used in Task 14?

Workform O: Summary of Investments Needed for Proposed Infrastructure

What outside assistance would be helpful in Task 14?

You may also wish to involve one or more staff members from the city or county budget office to join the committee for this task.

> *Enhanced level of effort:* This is a task that could be completed by an outside consultant with expertise in budgeting and fund-raising.

How long will Task 14 take?

It will probably take the committee members several weeks to research the funding options open to the library. The committee will review those options and make recommendations during one meeting.

What Should You Consider When Identifying Sources for the Funding Needed to Implement Your Plan?

When you finished Workform O: Summary of Investments Needed for Proposed Infrastructure and realized just how much money would be required to fully implement your proposed infrastructure and the purchase of the products and services you selected, you were probably somewhat startled by the total. The costs to implement a plan like this can add up quickly. However, it is important not to get discouraged by the total resources required. The library can obtain the needed resources from a variety of sources.

Reallocating Existing Resources

Libraries tend to assume that all new programs and services must be funded with new resources. However, in today's funding environment many libraries are realizing that to obtain the resources they need for new programs, they are going to have to reallocate funds from existing programs and services. All government funding is being scrutinized more carefully than ever before by taxpayers convinced that public services should be "leaner and meaner." Libraries are not exempt from this scrutiny, and, as librarians and board members know all too well, many public libraries are already operating with fewer resources than they need to accomplish everything they are being asked to do. This creates a very difficult situation for those responsible for obtaining and allocating the resources required to operate the library. There is no question that it is more pleasant to create new programs and services than it is to modify or discontinue programs that are no longer as effective as they once were.

If you have worked in your library for any length of time, you know that the library priorities have changed over the past decade or two as your community and its needs have changed. You may also know that the programs and services provided by the library have not always been modified to reflect the library's new priorities. If you choose to, you can use this technology planning process as the impetus for a full-scale review of all library operations. However, remember that it will be very difficult for you to evaluate your current resource allocations if you don't have a library service plan that identifies your priorities. You will also need to have some performance data about the services and programs you are evaluating.

Finally, you need to be very aware of the impact of the technology plan you have just completed on the current library services and programs. For example, if you have decided to provide on-line access to full-text periodicals, how will that affect your print periodicals budget? What is the impact of providing one or more encyclopedias in CD-ROM format? How should the fact that you decided to provide public access to the vast information resources available on the Internet affect your print nonfiction collection development? What about the impact of public access to the Internet on the expectations you have of your reference staff? We all know of libraries that have online catalogs and yet continue to maintain their paper card catalogs—some even continue to add to their accession books! When asked why, these libraries provide a variety of answers (most are versions of the old belt-and-suspenders story), but the real answer is that these libraries find it impossible to let go of the old when they implement the new. This is a luxury that libraries cannot afford as the pace of change accelerates and the cost of adapting to those changes increases. The libraries that succeed in this new environment will be those that replace and adapt their services and not the libraries that simply try to add endless new programs and services with no modification of their existing environment.

Requesting New Funds from Your Funding Body

It is unlikely that you will be able to fully implement your technology plan by reallocating your current resources, nor should you expect to do so. As you implement your technology plan, you will probably be making significant investments in equipment and software. You may also need to upgrade your facility(ies) to accommodate your selected technology infrastructure. Your first source of funding for many of these items will be your local funding body. Your funding body may more positively receive requests for funding for technology enhancements than they would other kinds of library requests. Sometimes it is difficult to convince people that additional funds are needed for materials or that you need new staff for a special program. However, the library is not the only local governmental agency that is being affected by technology. Many, if not most, of the other city or county departments are also automating their services. This is an area of expenditure that members of your funding body probably understand and recognize as inevitable.

Most governmental funding bodies provide two kinds of appropriations: one-time, or nonrecurring, appropriations and ongoing, or recurring, appropriations. When you prepare your budget request, you will want to think carefully about whether to request nonrecurring or recurring funds.

Nonrecurring Funds

In the past, many libraries have funded their automation purchases, both large and small, from one-time appropriations. However, as technology becomes integrated into every aspect of library service, that is no longer an appropriate funding strategy, any more than it would be to fund your materials budget with one-time monies.

What kind of expenditures should you make from one-time appropriations? It is certainly appropriate to fund building renovations, rewiring, cabling, etc., from one-time monies. It is also possible to purchase the basic computer furniture you need from nonrecurring funds. After all, the probable lifespan of the furniture is a lot longer than the probable lifespan of the equipment it will hold or the software that will run on the equipment. Finally, if one or more of your selected technology options requires a significant initial investment but can be maintained from a much smaller ongoing investment, it may be possible to make the initial investment from one-time monies, with the clear understanding that there will be ongoing costs associated with the project and that those will be budgeted from recurring funds.

Recurring Funds

Many of the costs associated with your technology plan would best be funded with recurring funds. Remember the study by the Gartner Group discussed in Task 10: Determine What It Will Cost to Implement the Proposed Infrastructure. That study found that the initial cost of owning PCs and other technology represents approximately 20 percent of the total cost of ownership. The other 80 percent of the cost comes from a variety of sources including installation, maintenance, training, and support. Furthermore, you will need to replace or upgrade your equipment and software regularly. Clearly, technology is an ongoing expense, just as your materials budget and staff costs are. You may want to work with representatives from your funding body to establish a new or expanded technology category in your operating budget if you don't have such a category now.

Using Funds Provided by Friends of the Library or Library Foundation

Many public libraries have library Friends groups that hold fund-raising activities and provide resources for special projects. More and more libraries are also establishing library foundations to manage fund-raising activities. Either of these groups could be a source of some of the funds you will need to implement your technology plan. However, if you intend to ask the Friends or foundation to support your plan, you will probably want to involve them in the process early on. You may not want to have a member of the Friends or the foundation board serve on the planning committee, and they probably won't want to spend that much time or be involved in that level of detail. However, you will want to keep them informed about the planning process and the decisions being made at each step of the process. By doing that, you will ensure that there are no surprises on either side. The Friends or foundation will have a clear understanding of what they are being asked to support because they have followed the process. That, in turn, should mean that the library will be able to rely on the funding to be available when it is needed.

The issues surrounding recurring and nonrecurring funds discussed in the previous sections also apply here. Some Friends groups or library foundations are quite able to commit to ongoing support for a project. Others rely on annual fund-raising activities, such as book sales or author dinners, and are more comfortable making one-time commitments. The way you spend the funds provided by Friends or a library foundation will depend on the type of funding available.

Obtaining Outside Grant Funds

A wide variety of grant opportunities are available to help libraries implement technology plans. The federal Library Services and Technology Act (LSTA), passed by Congress in 1996, focuses on helping libraries use technology to improve library services. The act has six priorities:

1. establishing or enhancing electronic linkages among or between libraries
2. electronically linking libraries with educational, social, or information services
3. assisting libraries in accessing information through electronic networks
4. encouraging libraries in different areas and encouraging different types of libraries to establish consortia and share resources
5. paying costs for libraries to acquire or share computer systems and telecommunications technologies
6. targeting library and information services to persons having difficulty using a library and to underserved urban and rural communities, including children (from birth through age 17) from families with incomes below the poverty line[1]

The Library Services and Technology Act provides funding to state library agencies in all fifty states, most of which in turn provide grants to libraries within their states. Every public library should be familiar with the grant opportunities available from their state library agencies. If you need further information you can call your state library agency or check its Web site. The Division for Libraries and Community Learning in Wisconsin maintains a Web listing of all fifty state library agencies at http://www.dpi.state.wi.us/www/statelib.html. For more information on the Library Services and Technology Act, check out the Web site maintained by the Institute of Museum and Library Services at http://www.imls.fed.us.

Many other grant opportunities are also available to help you implement your technology plan. When considering possible funding, it often pays to start at the local level. What local organizations or corporations might be interested in providing some of the resources you need? For example, you might want to ask the Lions Club for the funding you need to purchase special software for the visually impaired. A local corporation might be interested in supporting a literacy center or a job-skills program. Also, you may find that the Chamber of Commerce can help you find funding for providing technology-based services to your small-business community.

One of the most publicized national sources of grant monies for public library technology activities is the Gates Library Foundation, established in 1997 with a total endowment of more than $400 million. The guidelines for applying for Gates Library Foundation grants can be found at http://www.glf.org. Also, many other, lesser-known sources of grant funds are available to public libraries. The Corpus Christi Public Library has developed a Web page on funding sources on the Internet that you might find helpful as you try to identify possible funders (http://www.ci.corpus-christi.tx.us/ref/fundsite.htm). The site includes links to private foundations, government agencies that provide funding, and other sites of interest including several sites on grant writing.

Every potential funder will have different priorities and a different application process. The good news for you is that the technology plan you have developed using *Wired for the Future* should provide all of the information you need to complete any grant application you decide to submit. Just remember that the issues surrounding recurring and nonrecurring funds continue to apply here. Grant funders are very aware of the ongoing costs of projects, and one of the things they will be looking for in your application is a clear understanding of the appropriate uses of one-time funding and the ways that you intend to provide the necessary continuing support for the purchases made with grant funding.

Taking Advantage of Discounts and Special Rates

Another source of support for portions of your technology plan may be found in special or reduced rates on equipment, software, or telecommunications charges that are made available to public libraries. Many state public utility or public service commissions have passed special statewide telecommunication discounts for libraries and educational institutions. Check with your state library agency to see if any special state telecommunications discounts are available. Some equipment and software vendors also provide discounts for libraries and educational institutions. It never hurts to ask.

What Resources Other Than Money Would Be Useful?

Libraries often think of resources solely in terms of financial aid. However, there may be other kinds of resources that could be very valuable to you as you implement your technology plan. For example, if your building needs wiring or cabling, a local firm or contractor may be willing to do it for a reduced fee or as a civic contribution. Local computer stores may be willing to donate some hardware or software in return for public acknowledgment of their contribution. If you are operating with very limited funds, you may want to talk to the advanced woodworking class at your local high school about making computer tables.

Finally, consider asking for volunteers to help you introduce the public to any new technologies you install. For instance, when you make Internet access available to the public, you might recruit a group of experienced Internet users to help the staff during the critical first month or two.

The most important things to remember when looking for the resources to implement your technology plan are to be flexible and to be creative. It is also critical that you approach this task with a positive attitude. If you believe that there is no way you can fund the technology-based services and programs your library needs, you will be right—that kind of negative attitude is almost always a self-fulfilling prophecy. Focus, instead, on the positive. You have just completed a process that has resulted in a well-documented and fully justified plan for using technology to provide quality information services to the people of your community. This plan includes everything you need to make a compelling argument for support from your funding body and from outside grant providers, but you won't get what you need if you don't ask.

TASK 15
Develop an Implementation Time Line

In this task you will develop a time line for the installation of the infrastructure and for the acquisition of the products and services.

Who is responsible for Task 15?

The person selected to monitor the implementation (see Task 16: Monitor Implementation and Make Adjustments as Needed) may be asked to lead this task, or it can remain the responsibility of the planning committee chair. The library director and the planning committee chair will make this decision.

Who else is involved in Task 15?

The planning committee will help complete this task. If the person selected to monitor the implementation of the plan is not on the planning committee, he or she should be involved in this task. Other staff members with special expertise may be asked to assist the committee as well.

What data is needed for Task 15?

You will need to know what infrastructure investments you intend to make and the products/services you intend to buy. You will also need to understand what is required to install your selected infrastructure and products.

What workforms are used in Task 15?

Workform O: Summary of Investments Needed for Proposed Infrastructure
Workform Q: Selected Products/Services
Workform R: Technology Plan Implementation Stages
Workform S: Technology Plan Implementation Time Line

What outside assistance would be helpful in Task 15?

It is probable that you will have to get outside assistance to determine the specific activities required to implement your plan. This assistance will come primarily from the vendors of the hardware, software, and networks you plan to purchase.

How long will Task 15 take?

This task is time-consuming and may take as long as a month. The final implementation plans should be reviewed by the planning committee during its last meeting.

Who Should Be Responsible for the Implementation of the Plan?

One person within your organization should be given the responsibility for overall project management and coordination of the various stages and activities that need to be completed. That person, in consultation with library administration, should complete a copy of Workform R: Technology Plan Implementation Stages for each separate stage of the process to assist in tracking the project schedule. As an alternative to Workform R, a number of project-management software packages are available that can be used to plan and track the progress of multipart projects, for example, Project 98 (Microsoft), SureTrak Project Manager (Primavera Systems), and Project Scheduler (Scitor Corp.).

How Do You Know Where to Start?

As you know, your ability to use the products and services you have selected (listed on Workform Q: Selected Products/Services) is dependent on the implementation of the infrastructure. Therefore, implementation of your plan begins with acquiring and installing the components of your selected infrastructure that you identified on Workform O: Summary of Investments Needed for Proposed Infrastructure. The elements of your infrastructure will generally take longer to acquire, install, and test than the products will. The products normally arrive shortly after you order them. Developing the infrastructure may require coordinating the work of multiple tradespeople (such as electricians, building contractors, and telephone installers) in multiple sites as well as ordering, installing, and configuring the equipment.

Some of the infrastructure components you will acquire will be used with equipment or services you buy from other vendors. The most common examples of this are equipment you buy to work with telephone company services and the equipment and phone service you buy to link to an Internet service provider (ISP). Before you buy equipment to work with these third-party suppliers, be sure you know what services are available and which services you intend to use. For example, be sure your ISP can support ISDN telephone services before you contract for an ISDN Internet line from the phone company. If you choose frame relay services from the phone company for your internal WAN, you will need to specify frame relay communications equipment when you order your WAN hardware. Therefore, the first step in developing an implementation plan is to understand the technical parameters of your suppliers.

It will be easiest if you divide the implementation process into subsets or stages. Each of these stages will be further divided into the activities required to accomplish the stage, and each will take time to complete. Use a separate copy of Workform R: Technology Plan Implementation Stages to record your decisions for each stage of your implementation process.

To determine the time needed to implement your overall plan, you will need to determine the duration of the ordering, installation, and testing cycles for each of the stages of your plan. For example, if your first stage is site preparation, who will do the work—the city or county or an independent contractor? If it is an independent contractor, do you need to go to bid for those services, or do you simply have to schedule a time? How long is it likely to take to complete the site preparation in each location? (Ask potential suppliers to estimate this for you.) Allow time in your planning for staff to review and test the work. For site preparation this testing could mean counting data outlets, plugging equipment into electrical outlets, or reviewing test data the installer has produced. For phone lines, it may mean passing data over the line. It is also wise to allow a little time for fixing problems. It is a rare project that doesn't require a little cleanup at the end.

In addition to determining the duration of each stage of the implementation, you should decide which stages are dependent on the completion of other stages. For example, you can't install WAN equipment until you have telephone lines. Therefore, phone line installation is a prerequisite for WAN equipment installation. You can't use PCs unless you have electrical outlets to plug them into. Therefore, site preparation is a prerequisite for PC installation. If you determine that a stage has a prerequisite, add the duration of the prerequisite stage to the subsequent stage to determine the overall duration for that element. For example, figure 6 shows the sequence of ordering and installing WAN lines and equipment.

Charting the stages of your implementation on Workform S: Technology Plan Implementation Time Line will help you determine how long it will take to fully implement your plan. Workform S will also indicate the points in the implementation process at which you should be taking actions and what those actions are. Your general objective should be to schedule the installation of equipment, phone lines, and cabling and the beginning of product leases as close as possible to the time when you will begin productive use of them. This is particularly true of elements with ongoing costs such as phone services and product licenses. Paying for licenses for an Internet-based product before you have a functional Internet connection wastes money. Buying a number of PCs before you have the site preparation completed to use them means you will have to find a place to store them and may mean that by the time you start to use them they have been superseded by a later model.

FIGURE 6
Sample Project Schedule

	Wk. 1	Wk. 2	Wk. 3	Wk. 4	Wk. 5	Wk. 6	Wk. 7	Wk. 8
WAN phone lines Time to order Time to install								
WAN equipment Time to order Time to install								

Sometimes you don't have control over the timing of your implementation stages. For example, grant funds may have to be spent by a certain date even though unexpected delays in site preparation have delayed your project. However, the general questions to ask yourself as you are planning each stage are "When this stage is completed, will we be ready to use the product or service we have installed? If not, why not?" Is it because you missed a prerequisite? Is there another stage that must be completed at the same time for you to begin to use the product? You will want to take these interdependencies into account as you plan the implementation.

Can You Phase in the Implementation of Your Plan?

There are a number of reasons why you may want to implement your technology plan in phases. You may need to fund the total plan with money that will become available in multiple budget years. Perhaps your plan includes a significant amount of staff training, both for the public services staff and the staff members who will need to manage your technology, and you want to complete at least the first round of training before you begin to install new products. You may have a small staff that has time to master only one new product at a time or a technology staff that needs to learn to manage the first of the infrastructure investments you make before they can begin to manage additional infrastructure components. Whatever the reason, there are several ways you can phase in your technology plan. You can implement one product at a time or one facility at a time, or you can implement your plan at a minimal level of service and expand as funds become available or demand rises.

Installing One Product at a Time

This implementation model assumes that the full or nearly full infrastructure is in place and that your technology plan calls for an orderly extension of that infrastructure to support additional products and services over time. For example, you might already have a LAN. Your plan calls for you to add a CD-ROM server to that LAN and install one database or one family of databases with similar training requirements and user interfaces in that CD-ROM server. You train the staff and public to use the product and give your technical support staff time to learn how to support the LAN, the PC user workstations, and the CD-ROM databases. Once the initial stress of learning about the new technology has passed, additional databases can be introduced. You will find that the introduction of the second and subsequent databases will be easier, and the interval of time between introducing a new product and your staff's ability to absorb the next change will be reduced. Each subsequent product you introduce will use some of the skills learned for previous products.

Working in One Facility/Department at a Time

Sometimes the budget simply will not support the full implementation of the infrastructure at one time. Although you have been planning the infrastructure in its component parts, hardware and software, networks and training, it needs all the parts to operate. Buying the PCs without the network won't support shared resources; nor is there any point in installing an Internet connection without the PCs.

If you have a multibranch library, you might choose to phase in your technology plan one facility at a time. If your library is in a single building and you need to phase in the infrastructure, you can phase in by department. The only real exception to phasing within a building is the installation of electricity and data cabling and the increase in air conditioning, if necessary. When you hire electricians or building contractors to wire your building, the incremental cost of adding circuits or additional data cables is a fraction of the overall cost of the project. You should do the site preparation for the ultimate environment you intend to support, even if it may take you several years to implement all of your activities.

Installing the Minimum Required and Expanding Based on Demand

You can also phase in your plan based on growth as demand rises or money for workstations becomes available. This assumes that you can afford to implement all of the needed infrastructure components except the total number of end-user devices you expect to need. If you are introducing a new information product or service for the first time, it may take a while for your public to develop an interest (it probably won't, but it might). You can install the server (if needed), the network(s), and the products you have chosen; train the staff; then phase in the number of user workstations you offer as public usage grows. If you have done complete site preparation in each facility, adding workstations is a relatively simple process involving purchasing, configuring, and installing new equipment.

TASK 16
Monitor Implementation and Make Adjustments as Needed

Who is responsible for Task 16?

The person selected to monitor implementation of the technology plan is responsible for this task.

Who else is involved in Task 16?

Other staff members may be assigned responsibility for one or more stages of the implementation plan. The planning committee chair will assist the person selected to monitor the implementation process to identify "trigger-point" assumptions.

What data is needed for Task 16?

You will need to know what infrastructure investments you intend to make and the products/services you intend to buy. You will also need to understand what is required to install your selected infrastructure and products.

What workforms are used in Task 16?

Workform Q: Selected Products/Services
Workform R: Technology Plan Implementation Stages
Workform T: Trigger-Point Assumptions

What outside assistance would be helpful in Task 16?

As in Task 15, it is likely that this task will require the assistance of the vendors you have selected to provide the hardware, software, and networks.

How long will Task 16 take?

This task will continue until the hardware, software, and networks are installed, tested, and operational.

How Can You Effectively Monitor the Plan?

Technology changes so frequently it seems to defy a planning process. If in January you budget $2,000 to buy a 300 MHz Pentium II at the start of your next fiscal year in July, by the time the money becomes available to you, 300 MHz Pentium IIs may no longer be marketed. If your plan includes installing Logicraft's CD server software, Logicraft's product may be subsumed by Microtest's products if Microtest buys Logicraft in the interim. Databases that weren't on the Internet when you studied your options may be there by the time you get your infrastructure in place.

All of this will mean that implementing your technology plan will be a complex project. Acquiring the items listed in Workform Q: Selected Products/Services will not be a simple matter. It will not only involve making purchase decisions about rapidly changing equipment and services, it will also typically involve a number of different staff members, each responsible for one or more interdependent activities. Coordinating the work of multiple staff members and vendors to ensure that all of the stages and activities are completed on time and in the right order is crucial to success. That will be the primary responsibility of the project manager.

No matter how well you have planned, your implementation will take unexpected twists and turns. These will not occur because you didn't plan well but simply because the world of technology continued to move forward while you were gathering your resources and beginning your implementation. You need to build allowances for this into your implementation plan, especially if your plan covers multiple phases over multiple years.

When you have to make adjustments to your implementation plan, it will be helpful if you can review the critical assumptions that led to making the decision under review and determine if those assumptions are still true. For example, you may have decided to add a CD server in phase two, in addition to the Internet connection you installed in phase one, because a database you wanted was not available over the Internet. In that case, before you actually buy the CD server, it will be important to verify that your information about Internet availability is still true. Maybe you decided to buy fractional T1 phone lines for your WAN because you felt that full T1 lines were too expensive. By the time you are ready to actually make the purchase, the cost might have been reduced, or you might have more money available than you expected. If you become so focused on accomplishing each stage of your implementation plan that you don't review the underlying assumptions behind the activities, you may find yourself buying outdated technology or making decisions based on unwarranted financial restrictions.

To ensure that the assumptions are reviewed at the appropriate times, the project manager should identify these decision-confirmation points, or "trigger points," in the implementation plan before the implementation begins. Link each trigger point to a specific stage and activity on Workform R, and use Workform T: Trigger-Point Assumptions to record them. The project manager should work with the planning committee chair to list the assumptions for each trigger point now, while he or she can still remember them from the planning process. This will ensure that you remember to validate your assumptions as you proceed through your implementation.

What Do You Do When Conditions Change (and They Will)?

The most-common modifications you will experience in implementing your plan are changes in hardware configurations, software releases, and telecommunications costs. PCs and server configurations and prices change at least once every three months; software, especially commercial software packages such as Web browsers or security software like IKIOSK, are released in new versions every twelve to eighteen months. Phone companies are introducing new services at an astonishing rate. How can you cope?

One way is to stay flexible early in the implementation process. When planning for hardware purchases, rather than committing to a specific hardware configuration, identify the cost of the configuration you require and set that cost as the price you intend to pay. Use this price threshold in your budgeting process. Then, when the money becomes available and you actually purchase the equipment, get the best configuration you can (meeting your minimum requirements) at the price threshold you set. For example, you may think when you are applying for a grant that you intend to buy Pentium processors with 16MB of RAM; however, when you get ready to buy, the price you budgeted will buy Pentium II processors with 32MB of RAM. This commitment to a price rather than a configuration will keep you as current as possible with the technology, while also keeping you within the limits of your budget. Use this strategy in writing contracts with suppliers as well, especially if you are contracting for future deliveries. Describe your intended hardware purchases as the specific equipment "or better" in the body of your contracts. Describe software as "version X or later."

Although you want to stay abreast of developments in both hardware and software, it pays to be a little conservative in your willingness to adopt the latest technologies. When you are flirting with the cutting edge of technology, it is important to stay "behind the blade." Choose software in general usage, not in alpha or beta test releases, unless you have a compelling need for a feature in the test version. If you do choose a test version, remember that it *will* have problems and will require considerably more support than a more-stable, generally released version. The same is true of new hardware. The first release of a new computer chip needs a "shakedown" period, just like the first model year of a new automobile. Unless you enjoy troubleshooting problems, let someone else help the manufacturers work the bugs out of their new products.

Phone company services available for developing a WAN are in constant flux. It is more difficult and expensive, however, for you to change phone services than it is to change PC configurations. Your choice of phone company service dictates your WAN hardware selection. Once you have purchased WAN hardware, you are committed to a particular service until it becomes cost effective to make another choice. Even if you are implementing your WAN in phases over multiple years, you will want to stay with a single phone service and type of WAN hardware throughout your entire WAN. However, you still need to review your WAN decisions periodically. Every multiyear technology plan should have an annual trigger point to review your actual WAN costs and compare them against the costs of other options. When your comparison shows the costs of investing in new or upgraded WAN equipment is offset by the cost savings of adopting another form of service, it is time to consider changing your WAN services.

When Do You Start the Next *Wired for the Future* Process?

The implementation of the plan you just completed will take anywhere from six months to two or three years, depending on the complexity of the plan and your available resources. Then you will be right back where you were when you started this process—faced with having to make technology decisions with no plan upon which to base those decisions. Obviously, then, this plan is not the last technology plan you will ever need to write; it is the first in what will be an ongoing planning process.

You can approach this need for ongoing technology planning in a number of ways. Some libraries may choose to appoint a permanent technology review committee that will be responsible for keeping up with new ways to use technology to accomplish the library's desired outcomes and for working with the various sections within the library to identify new or evolving programs and services that might be supported using technology. Other libraries might prefer to appoint a new technology planning committee yearly after the library has updated its service plan and identified the activities for the upcoming year. Libraries with technology plans that require a multiyear implementation time line may choose to wait until the current plan is fully implemented before initiating another technology planning process.

However libraries choose to manage their ongoing technology planning, the process in *Wired for the Future* will serve as the framework for that planning. Libraries using this process will develop plans that use technology effectively to provide needed programs and services to the people in their communities.

NOTE

1. Library Services and Technology Act (1996). Available: http://www.imls.fed.us/mlsa.html (Mar. 1998).

Bibliography

Buildings, Books and Bytes: Libraries and Communities in the Digital Age. Benton Foundation, 1996. Available at http://www.benton.org/Library/Kellogg/ buildings.html. Mar. 1998.

Cheswick, William R., and Steven M. Bellovin. *Firewalls and Internet Security: Repelling the Wily Hacker.* Reading, Mass.: Addison-Wesley, 1994.

Derfler, Frank J., and Les Freed. *Get a Grip on Network Cabling.* Emeryville, Calif.: Ziff-Davis, 1993.

Dowd, Karen. *Getting Connected: The Internet at 56K and Up.* Sebastopol, Calif.: O'Reilly & Assoc., 1996.

Farley, Marc, Tom Stearns, and Jeffery Hsu. *LAN Times Guide to Security and Data Integrity.* Berkeley, Calif.: Osborne McGraw-Hill, 1996.

Himmel, Ethel, and William J. Wilson. *Planning for Results: A Public Library Transformation Process.* Chicago: American Library Association, 1998.

Hunt, Craig. *Networking Personal Computers with TCP/IP.* Sebastopol, Calif.: O'Reilly & Assoc., 1995.

LAN Tutorial. 3d ed. San Francisco: Miller Freeman, 1996.

Local Places, Global Connections. Np: Benton Foundation and Libraries for the Future, 1997.

Loshin, Pete. *TCP/IP for Everyone.* Boston: AP Professional, 1995.

Lowe, Doug. *Client/Server Computing for Dummies.* 2d ed. Foster City, Calif.: IDG Books, 1997.

McClure, Charles R., John Carlo Bertot, and John C. Beachboard. *Internet Costs and Cost Models for Public Libraries: Final Report.* Washington, D.C.: U.S. National Commission on Libraries and Information Science, 1995.

Nunemacher, Greg. *LAN Primer.* 3d ed. New York: M&T Books, 1995.

Orfali, Robert, Dan Harkey, and Jeri Edwards. *The Essential Client/Server Survival Guide.* 2d ed. New York: John Wiley and Sons, 1996.

Schatt, Stan. *Understanding Local Area Networks.* 4th ed. Indianapolis: Sams, 1993.

Sheldon, Tom. *LAN Times Encyclopedia of Networking.* Berkeley, Calif.: Osborne McGraw-Hill, 1994.

Tapscott, Don. *Growing Up Digital: The Rise of the Net Generation.* New York: McGraw-Hill, 1998.

Tech Notes

Building Wiring/ Data Cabling

When you finish reading this Tech Note, you will be able to

- identify the different types of wiring used to transmit data

- determine if your existing building wiring needs to be upgraded

- know where fiber optic cable might be of benefit in your network

- understand if you need a contractor to do your wiring and what standards to use for the wiring

Data networks are built on wires, also known as data cables, that pass data in the form of electrical signals between devices on the network. In the simplest of networks, a data cable running along the baseboard of a wall can be used to connect two or more PCs. (See figure 7.) In more-complex environments, the wire is installed in the walls, floors, or ceilings of a building, terminating in "data jacks" or plugs in the walls or floors, similar to telephone jacks or electrical outlets. (See figure 8.)

Most technology implementations that are meant to connect two or more devices require data cabling. Many libraries that automated in the 1970s and 1980s wired their buildings to connect character-cell "dumb" terminals to automated library systems using a type of data cable called **serial cable.** The technical specifications for data cable capable of carrying network traffic are very different from the specifications for serial cable. As library resources become more network based, even libraries that already have wire installed for an automated system are often faced with the need to rewire the building to support networked devices.

FIGURE 7
Simplest Network

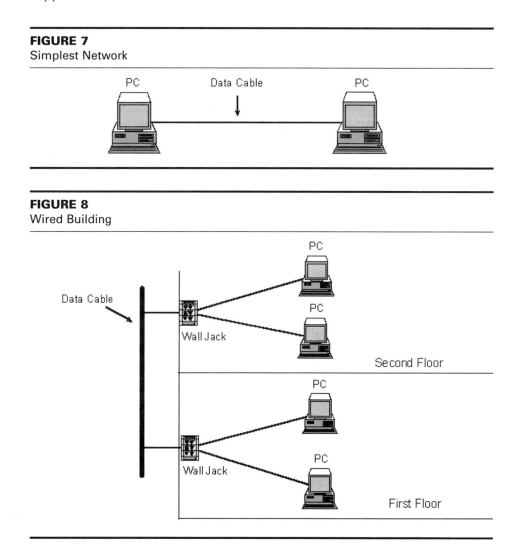

FIGURE 8
Wired Building

Protocols

Devices on networks can share data only if there is a common standard that all the devices observe for accessing the wire. Otherwise, multiple devices will try to send data at the same time, scrambling the messages. These standards are called **media access control (MAC) protocols.** The MAC protocols include specifications for the medium (type of wire), format, and speed of transmissions and how the medium is shared.

International organizations such as the Electronics Industry Association (EIA), the International Electrical and Electronics Engineers (IEEE), or the International Consultative Committee on Telephone and Telegraph (CCITT) publish MAC protocols that equipment and software manufacturers support in the products they develop, thus ensuring compatibility at the electrical signal level. The protocol most commonly supported in library applications is Ethernet. Some libraries may also have networks operating on the Token-Ring standard, an IBM proprietary standard, although this is less common. Two other standards, Arcnet and FDDI (Fiber Distributed Data Interface), are rarely used in public libraries.

Wire

Data cable is typically composed of one of two mediums: copper or glass fiber. The copper cables most commonly used for networks are coaxial cable, shielded twisted pair (STP), and unshielded twisted pair (UTP). The glass fiber cables, called **fiber optic cables,** use light instead of electrical pulses to carry data.

Coaxial cable consists of a copper center surrounded by a layer of insulation that is covered by copper braid or metallic foil. This is then covered by an outer cable jacket. The electrical circuit includes both the copper center and the copper braid or metallic foil, which means that both the center core and the braid must be properly connected to transmit the signal. Coaxial cable comes in two thicknesses: thick Ethernet cable that is nearly ½ inch in diameter and thinner coaxial cable, sometimes called thin Ethernet, that has an outside diameter of 0.18 inch. This thinner cable is more commonly used in library installations. When used in an Ethernet network, coaxial cable can transmit data at 10 million bits per second (Mbps).

Shielded twisted pair (STP) includes metal braid or foil around each pair or group of wires in the cable. This increases the thickness and the cost of the cable, but it provides better protection from ambient electrical interference (such as that created by fluorescent lights) that might disrupt the electrical pulses on the data cable. Unlike coaxial cable, the braid or foil is not a part of the electrical circuit, but the electrical grounding of STP cable is crucial. Improperly grounded STP cable is a common source of network problems. STP is specified by IBM for Token-Ring networks, although UTP can be used for Token Ring as well. The STP cable can also be used for Ethernet installations.

Unshielded twisted pair is the most commonly used medium in libraries for Ethernet installations. UTP is usually composed of two, three, or four pairs of electrical wires contained in a single cable jacket. The cable is thin and flexible, which makes it easy to install.

The Electronics Industry Association/Telecommunications Industry Association (EIA/TIA) has published standards for network cables (EIA/TIA-568 and 569) that include performance and installation specifications for five different categories of cable. Data cable is usually distinguished by these categories.

Category 1 cable contains untwisted wire and is not recommended for data transmission.

Category 2 cable is appropriate for Apple Talk networks and as wiring for IBM 3270 terminals and IBM AS/400 systems.

Category 3 is the lowest category of cable for use in Ethernet networks. It will work effectively in Ethernet networks transmitting at 10 Mbps or in Token-Ring networks transmitting at 4 Mbps. Category 3 cable is the cable commonly used for voice telephone transmissions.

Category 4 cable is rated to transmit Token-Ring data at 16 Mbps and Ethernet traffic at 10 Mbps.

Category 5 cable can be used to transmit Ethernet signals at 100 Mbps. It will also handle Token Ring at 16 Mbps and Ethernet at 10 Mbps. For this reason, category 5 is the most commonly used cable in new installations today. Category 5 cable must have four pairs of wires to conform to the standard.

Fiber optic cable is available in single mode and multimode. Single mode fiber transmits signals over long distances and is more expensive than multimode. Single mode fiber is usually used to connect buildings in private wide area networks (WANs). The fiber optic cable most commonly used for building wiring is multimode fiber. Installing fiber is a highly specialized skill; therefore, it is more expensive than UTP installations. The most common use of fiber in a building is as "vertical wiring," connecting multiple floors of a building, rather than as "horizontal wiring," connecting devices to hubs. Because the light pulses on fiber cable are not subject to electrical interference in the same way that electrical pulses are, fiber is sometimes used in "noisy" areas that have the potential for electrical interference with data signals. Ethernet signals transmitted over fiber can travel at 100 Mbps.

Connectors

Wiring a network includes more than just the physical wire itself. The wire must be terminated at each end with connectors that allow it to be connected to a personal computer, network server, hub, or other piece of network equipment. The terminating connector for UTP is an eight-position plug, also commonly called an RJ-45 plug. The connector that terminates a coaxial cable is a BNC connector, a round connector that snaps or screws into place. It is important that the connector on the device and the connector on the data cable be compatible. If they are not, a device called a **transceiver** can be used to translate between incompatible wiring connections.

Installation

Simple networks of a few nearby devices can be installed by library staff using premade Category 5 UTP cables. The cables are available in varying lengths from mail order sources and local computer stores. Larger, building-wide projects will require the skills of trained installers familiar with the EIA/TIA-568 and 569 specifications and the fire codes and building codes of the community. Whether the data cabling is done by staff or contractors, each end of every cable should be clearly labeled with a labeling scheme that permits easy identification of both ends of each wire.

Unless special building needs or automation system vendor requirements dictate otherwise, Category 5 UTP wiring is an appropriate cabling standard for libraries to adopt. It provides a good balance between cost and utility and will support the networked services most commonly offered by public libraries, including CD-ROM databases, Internet access, and local automation systems.

Additional Resources

Further information on network wiring can be found in the following sources.

Barton, John E. "Growing the Right Cable Plant." *Network Computing* 708 (15 May 1996). Available at http://www.techweb.com.

Derfler, Frank J., and Les Freed. *Get a Grip on Network Cabling.* Emeryville, Calif.: Ziff-Davis, 1993.

Jones, James. "A Practical Guide to Fiber." *LAN* 12, no. 4 (Apr. 1997): 77–80. Available at http://www.network-mag.com.

Raynovich, R. Scott. "Networks Set Up to Bulk Up on Beefier Cable." *LAN Times* (11 Sept. 1995). Available at http://www.lantimes.com.

Trulove, James. *LAN Wiring.* New York: McGraw-Hill, 1997.

Wryden, Nick. "Get Wired." *Communications Week* 642 (16 Dec. 1996).

The following is a good source of definitions for the terms you will encounter in working with vendors.

Shnier, Mitchell. *Dictionary of PC Hardware and Data Communications Terms.* Sebastopol, Calif.: O'Reilly & Assoc., 1996.

Florida Community College at Jacksonville offers course notes for several basic courses, including "Basic Networking Concepts" and "Network Wiring Basics" on its Web server at http://indy.fccj.cc.fl.us/lsf/CDA2502.html.

Character/Packet Data

When you finish reading this Tech Note, you will be able to understand

- how networked information differs from character-based data

- why and how that difference affects a library's technology planning

All electronic data passed across wires is represented as electrical pulses. This is true whether the wire is data cabling in your building or telephone wire connecting remote sites. With fiber optic cables, the representation of data is in pulses as well, but on fiber the pulses are light pulses rather than electrical pulses.

Character-Based Protocol

The only way devices can share data over a wire is by agreeing on a standard for how the pulses will represent the data. These agreements are called **protocols.** There are a large number of protocols that have been defined as standards for sharing data. Among the earliest of the protocols was the **asynchronous byte-oriented** or **character-based protocol.** In this protocol, each character in a string of text is represented to a computer by a particular combination of eight electrical pulses, or **bits.** Each set of eight bits equals one **byte** or one character of data. The eight bits of data are surrounded by one start bit (at the beginning) and one stop bit (at the end) to tell the computer where the actual data begins and ends. This protocol is the basis for most communication between dumb terminals and computers.

Packet Protocol

Most of the library automation systems installed in the 1970s, 1980s, and early 1990s used this character-based protocol to transmit information between a library's terminals and its central computer. As networks of computers evolved, however, new protocols were developed to support data transfer in packages of information, called **packets,** rather than one character at a time. Packets contain data and headers. The amount of data varies, but it can be as much as 1,500 bytes or almost a full page of information. The headers include both the address of the sending computer and the address of the destination computer as well as certain control data that ensure that the packet arrives at its destination without errors. The use of packets allows more data to be sent per unit of time over a given communication medium. Packets are possible because even the simplest of networked devices have some computing power and are capable of assembling and disassembling the packages of data. Standards, also called protocols, were developed that determined how data packets would be assembled for passing between networked machines.

Today, most new installations of multidevice systems in libraries are based on networks and packet data transfer. This is true even when the desktop machines are dumb terminals because usually the dumb terminals are wired to a device called a **terminal server,** which translates the character-based protocol of the terminals to packets before it sends the data to the central computer. The terminal server also disassembles the packets returned by the central computer to character protocol before sending the data to the terminal screen.

Conversion

Character-based protocols were used in early library automation systems because they were less expensive. These systems used dumb terminals, not intelligent devices, to communicate. Character-based protocols have less stringent wiring requirements for the quality of the wire used to pass data; they can also use less complex telecommunications equipment to pass data over telephone lines.

Unfortunately, now that many library resources are accessed from the Internet or from networked CD-ROMs or PC hard drives, the limitations of the character-based protocols are becoming obvious. Networked CD-ROMs and PC files designed for sharing assume the presence of a packet network. Although it is possible to access Internet resources at character-based devices by using a special software program called Lynx, the Internet is a graphically oriented environment and reducing it to a character-based world loses much of its richness and value and much of its ease of use. Libraries that want to offer access to graphical resources but still have wiring and telecommunications links to remote sites based on character protocols need to upgrade their wiring and communications devices to be able to pass packet traffic between networked devices.

For libraries with a large population of dumb terminals that can't be replaced, investing in terminal servers makes it possible to include the terminals in the packet network. Most library automation vendors offer their customers this option. It is important, however, to balance the cost of the terminal servers against the cost of replacing the terminals. Often, if a remote site has three or fewer desktop devices, it is less expensive to replace the terminals with PCs than it is to buy a terminal server.

You don't have to wait until you can afford to convert everything before you begin. It is possible to migrate from a completely character-based environment to a packet-based network in stages. Networks can be designed that handle a mix of character-based terminals and networked PCs. If you don't have the skills within your staff to plan a complete or phased migration to packet networking, seek help from your library system vendor, a telecommunications consultant, or one of your other sources for technical assistance.

Client Server Computing

When you finish reading this Tech Note, you will be able to

- define client server computing

- understand how it is applied in library applications

- determine if a client server system is needed or appropriate for a product or service you are considering

The first widespread use of technology in public libraries was for online circulation control and public access catalog systems in the 1970s. These systems were host-based systems, which means they had centrally located computers that had all the programming on them and did all the data manipulation and storage centrally. The user devices for these host-based systems were character-based terminals, which we now call "dumb" terminals. The terminals had no processing capacity; they could accept only characters of data from the host and display them on a screen.

Today, with the availability of personal computers and networks, a model of computing has developed called **client server computing.** At its most basic, client server computing divides a computer application into three parts: a client machine, a server machine, and a network that connects the two. The two machines share in some fashion the running of the application program.

Client server computing evolved from a software development strategy called modular programming. With modular programming a large piece of software was broken down into smaller discrete programs called **modules.** Each module was easier to program and maintain. For example, separate modules were developed for managing the input or display of data on a screen or managing the storage of data on a disk drive or magnetic tape. A client module sends a message to a server module requesting that the server perform some task or service. Originally these modules were all run on the same computer using the same computer memory for their execution. As networks were developed that allowed two or more computers to be connected, programmers began to realize that there was no reason why the modules of a program necessarily had to run in the same set of computer memory. Thus began the evolution of the **client server architecture,** which is two or more computers connected by a network.

Today most librarians think of client server computing as a desktop PC with a graphical user interface (GUI) interacting via a network with a data source, such as an integrated library system or a CD-ROM tower, to retrieve, display, and update data. While this is a commonly held belief by librarians, it is not necessarily what library vendors mean by client server. Some library automation vendors whose systems clearly use dumb terminals will tell you they have always had a client server system. What they mean is they have always employed modular programming techniques. Some networks have dumb servers, machines that are used only to centrally store files for other computers in the network or machines whose only function is to manage a printer that is shared by other computers on the network. These servers are not actually participating in the maintenance of the data. In fact, the computer industry generally recognizes several different models of networked machines as client server computing.

Most library applications consist of three elements: the user interface, the database, and the "business logic," or programming that dictates how users can manipulate the data in the database. (A circulation control application is an example of business logic.) The **user interface,** or client, dispatches requests to the server and manages the display of data to the user. The **server** responds to requests received from the client, executes database retrievals, and manages data integrity, which is particularly important in an integrated library system where the circulation, cataloging, and acquisitions staff may all be accessing the same records at the same time for different purposes. The business logic, or programming, can be included in the client, in the server, or in a separate set of programs that work between the client and the server. When an application consists of clients and/or servers that contain the business logic, it is called a **two tier application.** When the business logic is written separately and interfaces with both the client and the server, the application is referred to as a **three tier application.** Many library applications introduced in the mid-1990s and later are being described by their developers as three tier applications.

Types of Client Servers

There are basically three types of client server implementations:

- the business logic running on the server with the client handling only the presentation of the data, sometimes referred to as the **remote presentation model**
- the business logic running on the client with the server providing only database storage and retrieval, the **remote processing model**
- the business logic distributed between the client and the server, or the **distributed functions model**

These three types do not represent distinct product designs, however. Think of them as three points along a continuum of client server implementations. A client server application may have elements of more than one type of implementation.

server-based applications   client-based applications   distributed applications

A library product that is marketed as a client server product can employ one, two, or all three of these techniques. A vendor's circulation module may employ a remote presentation design, the technical services workstation might be a remote processing application, and the online catalog could be a distributed function implementation. This is especially true in systems that are migrating incrementally from an older text-based host and terminal design to a client server design.

Remote Presentation Model

The remote presentation model of client server means the vendor develops a graphical user front end for a traditional text-based application. The application itself may remain unchanged; only the screens the user sees and interacts with are changed. Most integrated library systems vendors adopted this model as their first step into client server architecture. Most of the text-based CD-ROM database vendors used this approach as well.

Remote Processing Model

A remote processing model means that the application processing takes place on the client; the server is used primarily for database retrieval and storage. The client requests a file or a group of records from the server and then works with that data using the business logic contained in the client application. When the client is done manipulating the data, it is returned to the server for storage. Office automation networks, such as Novell networks, are examples of this type of client server implementation. Many CD-ROM networks, with the CDs in a tower accessible by a number of PCs, are remote processing client server implementations; the application for requesting, sorting, and printing the data is loaded on every PC, and only the data on the CD itself is shared over the network. Library vendors' systems with specialized user software for particular functions, such as a technical services client application, often employ the remote processing model for these functions.

Distributed Functions Model

Distributed function client server applications are the most complex to build and administer. In this type of application, the software developer needs to decide which of the two, client or server, is better suited to perform a particular function and write the application accordingly. Because the business logic of the application is distributed between client and server, the two generally need to be developed and maintained by the same supplier.

Java-based applications are a special form of distributed functions, allowing developers to distribute functions to the client through **applets,** or small programs, that are downloaded by the server to the client to be run. (Java is a specialized programming language created to develop network-based applications.) In the case of Java-based applications, the client and the server do not need to be developed by the same supplier as long as both adhere to the same Java standards. Some, but not all, library vendors are beginning to employ Java features in their systems. Java is neither better nor worse for library applications than other programming languages; it is just another approach vendors can take to developing their applications.

Implications

Why do any of these distinctions matter to a library? If you are planning to buy a stand-alone integrated system or CD-ROM network from a single vendor who will install and support the product throughout its useful lifetime, the distinctions in the forms of client server are probably not important to you. As long as the product meets your needs and the vendor supports it, it won't matter. But if you intend to integrate a variety of products from multiple vendors on a local area network (LAN) or wide area network (WAN) or to share data with other departments in your city or county, the types of client server applications you are installing will matter. Each type of client server application makes different demands on a network's capacity to transmit data. Remote presentation implementations typically transfer just character data between client and server; remote processing implementations pass entire files requiring more capacity, or **bandwidth,** to support them. Distributed function applications, whether custom programs or Java applets, will have varying bandwidth requirements, depending on the amount and type of data the application transfers. If you intend to implement a client server application, it is important that the requirements of the application for data transfer do not exceed the capacity of your network.

Why Use a Client Server System?

Client server software design allows an organization to distribute processing power from the server to the desktop. This means a business with PCs on every desk can use some of that desktop processing power to meet its data processing needs rather than investing in bigger and more powerful servers. But public libraries don't usually have a large population of underused PCs on the desktops, so this isn't a compelling argument for a client server design in most public libraries.

However, more and more library materials are becoming available in electronic format and are being distributed from a variety of networked sources, including CD towers on LANs and vendors' servers on the Internet. With few exceptions, these resources are not accessible by dumb terminals, so libraries are having to invest in desktop PCs to gain access to them. The public is also becoming more familiar with PCs in their offices and at home, especially with graphical user interfaces (GUI) such as Windows or Macintosh OS, and their expectations for how computer-based systems should look are changing. The same public that used a character-based interface for the online catalog for the last ten years now perceives it as difficult to use because they expect the same GUI/mouse-driven interface they have on the other computers they use. Children who have never known anything other than Windows and the Web are particularly challenged by text-based terminal interfaces.

In this multiple resource/GUI world, the primary benefit of client server computing in a public library is in being able to access multiple resources with a single client. If every electronic database a library chose to license had its own user interface, and therefore its own application software that had to be loaded on a client machine before the database could be used, the costs of managing the clients would increase with each new resource added. Choosing resources that can be accessed by a single client, usually a Web browser, means that library staff can concentrate on using the information in the resource, not administering the clients that access it.

Fat Clients and Thin Clients

Much has been written about "fat clients" and "thin clients" in client server implementations. **Fat clients** are used in remote processing applications, where the business logic for how to use and manipulate the data is included in the client programming. **Thin clients** are presentation managers that interpret data received from a server and display it on the user's machine. A basic World Wide Web browser is an example of a thin client.

Fat clients can be expensive to manage. Deploying fat clients to multiple desktops in a library means that each machine must be updated whenever the client software changes. Each time a vendor delivers a new version of a graphical client application for staff or the public, that client must be distributed to each desktop machine using that client. Fat clients also tend to make desktop machines obsolete. As an application grows in complexity and functionality, it often requires more memory or a faster processor to continue to deliver acceptable performance.

With thin clients, changes to the application are made on the server side, making it much easier and more cost effective to introduce changes to a large population of users. Although the application's complexity may increase and require more computing power to operate, it will be primarily the server that is affected; the desktop thin clients will continue to operate without an upgrade.

Although a basic Web browser can be thought of as a thin client, Web browsers are not all that "thin" as used by most public libraries. Because a library's browser is usually an access tool used to gather information from a wide variety of sources, the typical library browser supports launching a wide variety of **helper applications.** These helper applications, usually loaded on the client machine, are needed to retrieve and view the various files found at Web sites. For example, an Adobe Acrobat reader is needed to retrieve and print tax forms from the IRS; a sound application such as Real Audio is needed to retrieve sound files from the Library of Congress American Memory pages. Telnet and FTP applications are needed for many sites as well. (See the Tech Note on Communications Protocols and TCP/IP Services for a description of Telnet and FTP.) Because of the security issues a library faces with public access technology—protecting the operating system and hard drive of a public access computer from malicious or inadvertent damage, for example—even a basic browser is often supplemented with machine-specific security software. This is another step from thin to fat.

Operating Systems

Client server systems are based on networks. The fundamental assumption of any client server system is that multiple clients are sharing access to a set of common resources, whether those resources are machine readable files, such as a library's circulation and OPAC databases, or physical resources, such as a networked printer or a router to connect to the Internet.

There are two types of networks, peer-to-peer networks and client server networks. In **peer-to-peer networks,** each networked computer (node) runs an operating system with built-in networking support that allows the nodes to share resources. In a **client server network,** a network operating system manages the sharing of resources. The most common network operating systems in libraries are UNIX (including Sun's Solaris), Novell's NetWare, and Windows NT. (See the Tech Note on Network Operating Systems for more information.)

There are some benefits to client server computing for public libraries, especially as the breadth of electronic resources used to deliver basic services increases. However, there are also increased costs for desktop PCs to replace dumb terminals. The technical details are not as important as the end user. Pick an operating environment that makes your users comfortable and applications that meet your service objectives, and get on with it.

Additional Resources

Greshenfeld, Nancy. "Client-Server: What Is It? Are We There Yet?" *Online* 19 (Mar./Apr. 1995): 60–4.

LAN Tutorial. 3d ed. San Francisco: Miller Freeman, 1996.

Lazar, Bill. "Client Server Moves to the 'Net.'" *LAN* 11, no. 8 (Aug. 1996): 107–12.

Lowe, Doug. *Client/Server Computing for Dummies.* 2d ed. Foster City, Calif.: IDG, 1997.

Nance, Barry. "Client/Server Versus Web Server Development." *Network Computing* 8, no. 6 (1 Sept. 1997): 130–3.

Orfali, Robert, Dan Harkey, and Jeri Edwards. *The Essential Client/Server Survival Guide.* 2d ed. New York: John Wiley and Sons, 1996.

Communications Protocols and TCP/IP Services

When you finish reading this Tech Note, you will be able to

- identify various communications protocols

- understand why you need to know the differences among the protocols

- identify the functions of the TCP/IP services used by libraries

Protocols are sets of rules for communicating between computers. *Protocol* is also one of the most overused words in network terminology. It is sometimes very hard to sort out which types of protocol a particular article, book, or speaker is referencing when the term is used. As it is used in this Tech Note, *protocol* means "the agreed-upon set of rules two devices use to transmit data to each other over a network connection."

In the Network Equipment Definitions Tech Note, the protocols supporting the physical transfer of data and the Open Systems Interconnect (OSI) model are discussed. In this Tech Note, we are discussing the protocols used at layer 4 of the OSI model, the transport layer. The transport layer is responsible for ensuring that data is successfully sent and received between two network devices. If data is lost or damaged in transmission, the protocols operating at the transport layer detect the problem and ask for retransmission of the data.

Communications Protocols

The layer 4 protocols most widely used in libraries today are TCP/IP (Transmission Control Protocol/Internet Protocol), Novell's IPX/SPX (Internet Packet Exchange/Sequenced Packet Exchange), and Microsoft's NetBEUI. (IP and IPX are actually layer 3 protocols, but that distinction isn't important for understanding protocols sufficiently to develop your library's technology plan.) TCP/IP is used with integrated library systems based on the UNIX operating system and the Internet. IPX/SPX is used in office automation or CD-ROM networks based on the Novell operating system. NetBEUI is frequently the protocol implemented in Windows-based local area networks, especially Windows for Workgroups and Windows 95 networks. NetBEUI can also be used in Windows NT-based networks, although most library implementations of Windows NT use TCP/IP. Because NetBEUI is limited to use on a local area network (it can't be handled by routers), special implementations of NetBEUI have been developed to run over TCP/IP so that it can be routed. (See the Tech Note Network Equipment Definitions for information on routing.)

The most important thing to understand about protocols is that all the devices in a network must agree to support a single protocol to share data. A PC that is putting IPX/SPX packets on a network data cable cannot use those packets to communicate with a server expecting to receive TPC/IP data. Nor can a Novell server running IPX/SPX share files with a PC that supports only NetBEUI.

A PC or server prepares data to be transmitted over a network by passing that data to its network interface card (NIC). Software called a **protocol stack** determines how to package the data before using the NIC to send data over the network data cable. If multiple protocol stacks have access to the NIC, the application that is sending the data determines which protocol stack to use in packaging the data. Although servers generally support only one protocol, client PCs may support multiple protocol stacks, depending on the number and types of servers with which they expect to communicate. For example, a PC that accesses both CDs on a Novell network and the Internet will need to support both IPX/SPX and TCP/IP.

A network can be designed to support multiple protocols over a single set of data cabling, but this can be a very complex environment to set up, manage, and troubleshoot. As a result, most libraries that have networks using multiple protocols have physically separated the data cabling for each network. A Novell network used for administrative functions is usually completely separate from the TCP/IP network used with the library's integrated library system. As a library's need for integrating multiple data resources (local system, CD-ROMs, Internet, etc.) increases, however, this separation becomes less acceptable. Libraries need to either integrate their multiple protocols into a single physical network or standardize their networked applications to use a single protocol. Since a single protocol environment is easier to set up and support, most libraries choose to standardize on a single protocol. Because the Internet is so integral to modern library service, most libraries choose to standardize on TCP/IP, the protocol of the Internet, as their communications protocol.

Fortunately, libraries are not the only institutions that are heavy users of the Internet. Companies like Novell are integrating their products with the TCP/IP protocol to ensure that they have a place in a networked future that will most assuredly be heavily biased toward TCP/IP.

TCP/IP Services

When the UNIX operating system and TCP/IP were developed in the 1970s and early 1980s, commercial PC programs were not as common as they are today. Part of the development of TCP/IP included the development of certain applications that were used to access and operate on the data the TCP/IP networks shared. These applications are still with us today, although the client side of these applications has often been wrapped into modern graphical user interface programs that don't look much like the original programs did.

The most commonly known TCP/IP services (also sometimes called protocols) include FTP, Gopher, HTTP, SMTP/POP/MIME, SNMP, and Telnet.

FTP   **File transfer protocol** (FTP) is really two programs, a client and a server (called in UNIX parlance a *daemon*). The client program contacts the server, searches the directories of available files, and copies entire files from the server's storage to the client. Alternately, with the right permissions a client can use FTP to put a file on a server. Access to the server's files can be controlled by user IDs and passwords, or the server can offer "anonymous FTP" permitting any client to download publicly available files from the server. Software companies often use FTP as a way for users to get updates to licensed software packages over the Internet.

Gopher   Gopher is an application developed by the University of Minnesota to make accessing files on a remote system a bit more user friendly. Instead of needing to know the UNIX commands to change directories and find files you might wish to download, Gopher supports organizing file directories as a series of menus.

HTTP   **Hypertext transfer protocol** (HTTP) defines how World Wide Web (WWW) servers and WWW clients (browsers) interact to transfer data. If a library is using its vendor's Web-based online catalog inside its facilities or on the Internet or has a Web server located in the library for serving its own pages to the Internet, it is using HTTP.

A **Web server** is a piece of software that resides on a computer and is used to organize Web pages and respond to incoming HTTP requests to see those Web pages. Web servers can also execute special scripts (small programs called **CGI scripts** [common gateway interface]) that permit them to retrieve and display non-Web data in the form of Web pages. This is the strategy used when a "Web front end" is used with a Z39.50 database. (See the Z39.50 Tech Note for more information.)

SMTP/POP/MIME

Simple mail transport protocol (SMTP) is the TCP/IP protocol used for exchanging electronic mail. The sender writes an electronic mail message and uses SMTP to deliver it directly to the addressee. This works fine if both the sender's machine and the receiver's machine are turned on and connected to the network when the message is sent. However, in the case of Internet e-mail, this is rarely the case.

Most Internet electronic mail is actually sent from client machines to special software programs called **mail servers.** These servers store received mail for their users until the users are ready to request their e-mail. Mail servers must have a full-time connection to the Internet to receive mail because there is no way to predict when an electronic message might arrive. This is why most dial-up Internet accounts come with e-mail service from the Internet service provider (ISP), because the ISP has a live full-time connection to the Internet.

Although it is possible to connect to a mail server via a text-based mail reader such as Pine or Elm to read mail stored on the mail server, most users prefer to download their mail to their own PC before reading, replying, and filing it. (Pine and Elm are commonly available on UNIX machines and used by some library integrated system vendors to supply internal staff e-mail systems.) The **post office protocol** (POP) is used to transfer mail from a mail server to a user's own machine. Both the mail server and the mail client must support POP to effect the transfer of e-mail.

The **multipurpose Internet mail extensions** (MIME) permit users to attach entire files to electronic mail messages. This makes it easy to transfer large messages between e-mail accounts or to attach nontext data, such as pictures, spreadsheets, or sound clips, to an e-mail message. The entire text of *Wired for the Future* was developed by the authors passing it between each other over the Internet as MIME attachments to e-mail messages.

SNMP   **Simplified network management protocol** (SNMP) provides a standard framework that designers of networks can use to develop network monitoring and management tools. As networks have come to cover wider and wider areas, it has become increasingly clear that physically visiting a device to troubleshoot it is not an effective management technique; it is both too time consuming and too costly.

SNMP standards make it possible to monitor a network's performance statistics and change the state of certain network devices. Changing the state of a device can range from ending a running program to rebooting the device. To use SNMP, a library needs a software package that will collect, analyze, and display SNMP data, as well as network devices that are capable of capturing, storing, and forwarding SNMP data upon request. The difference between managed and unmanaged hubs is this ability to produce SNMP data. A managed hub has the capacity to do so, although the software needed may be an option, and an unmanaged hub does not. (See the Network Equipment Definitions Tech Note for more information about hubs.) Very few library vendors have included SNMP in their integrated systems as a standard feature or even an option. Understanding how to analyze and use SNMP data is a specialized skill. Libraries that don't have that skill available to them will probably be able to use SNMP only if they hire a vendor to monitor or manage their network.

Telnet   When data first became accessible to online users (as opposed to batch processing programs on computers that created printed output), most users interacted with computers via terminals. When users began to access multiple computers, they didn't want to have multiple terminals on their desks, so software was developed that allowed a user to access multiple computers from a single terminal. The user was usually connected to his or her primary system via a terminal connected by a data cable. To connect to another system, the user's primary system established a connection on behalf of its user through a program called Telnet. Originally, Telnet was an application that ran on a computer on behalf of a user at a terminal. It has also evolved to be a PC-based software application as PCs have become more widespread.

Like the other TCP/IP services, Telnet is really two programs: a Telnet server application that runs on the server machine and a Telnet client application running on the desktop PC. The Telnet client takes keyboard commands from the user and translates them into a set of universal commands. The Telnet server software receives these universal keyboard commands and translates them into the keyboard commands the application on that particular server machine is expecting to receive. When the server sends data to the client, the process is reversed.

Additional Resources

Chae, Lee. "Lesson 103: E-Mail and SMTP." *Network Magazine*. 1997. Online. Available at http://www.networkmagazine.com/tutors/9703tut.htm. 4 Feb. 1998.

———. "Lesson 106: The Basics of E-Mail Access." *Network Magazine*. 1 June 1997. Online. Available at http://www.networkmagazine.com/tutors/9706tut.htm. 4 Feb. 1998.

Dowd, Kevin. *Getting Connected: The Internet at 56K and Up*. Sebastopol, Calif.: O'Reilly & Assoc., 1996.

Hunt, Craig. *Networking Personal Computers with TCP/IP*. Sebastopol, Calif.: O'Reilly & Assoc., 1995.

LAN Tutorial. 3d ed. San Francisco: Miller Freeman, 1996.

Liu, Crickett, and others. *Managing Internet Information Services*. Sebastopol, Calif.: O'Reilly & Assoc., 1994.

Loshin, Pete. *TCP/IP for Everyone*. Boston: AP Professional, 1995.

Steinke, Steve. "Lesson 102: Simple Network Management Protocol—SNMP." 1997. Online. Available at http://www.networkmagazine.com/tutors/9702tut.htm. 4 Feb. 1998.

Computer and Network Security

When you finish reading this Tech Note, you will be able to understand

- how to secure a PC from four different security risks
- what steps you can take to protect your library's database
- how a firewall can, and can't, protect your data
- how to administer a good password system

Securing a library's automated hardware and software resources from harm is an important issue. The money and time invested in even a small installation of PCs needs to be protected from inadvertent or malicious damage. However, different threats require different responses, and not all available solutions are appropriate or effective for libraries. After all, much of a library's investment in technology is meant to be used by the general public, by anyone who walks through the door of the building or connects to the library's Web server. The security challenges of a public access environment are quite different from those faced by private enterprise, or even other public agencies, where the assets to be protected are meant to be accessible to a limited number of users.

In developing any plans for security, the two key questions are "What are we trying to protect?" and "Who are we trying to protect it from?" You must answer these two questions before you can evaluate the potential effectiveness of any proposed security solution. Although there are many commercial products that can be quite valuable in protecting library technology assets, unfortunately there are also a number of products installed in libraries today that do not provide the protection the librarians thought they were buying. All too often vendors of security solutions, parent agency management information system (MIS) staff, and even security consultants do not understand the unique nature of the public access environment. Nor do they understand that the library's mission is to provide access to its databases, not to protect them from use.

Libraries need to concern themselves with several levels of security, depending on the computing environment they operate. At the most-basic level, the user workstations you offer to the staff and public must be protected from configuration changes that can interrupt their operation, including the theft of key devices such as computer mice. Your electronic resources, especially dynamic files such as your online catalog and circulation databases, must be protected from unauthorized users trying to affect the data files. A network that includes both internal and external files and servers must be configured to ensure that internal resources are not available to external users. Each of these concerns requires a different response.

PC Security

PCs and their software were designed as single-user systems. The assumption is that the authorized user is a trusted person with his or her own PC and applications that are solely his or hers to use. That is not the case with public access PCs in libraries. There are four levels of security risks on a PC that libraries need to understand. Some of the security options discussed in the following sections are appropriate for every PC in a library. Others have to be considered in light of the intended use of the PC. For example, you can't block access to the floppy drive or disallow access to the Save function in an application if you intend to let library users save data to floppy disks.

Physical Security

The first level and most-basic protection public access PCs need is physical protection. PCs should be located in visible high traffic areas under line-of-sight control of staff, not stuck in an out-of-the-way corner where a hacker would have all the time in the world to crack your security. The system unit itself should be isolated as much as possible from the patrons. Some libraries use furniture that places the system unit inside a lockable enclosure. Ideally, users should not be able to access the power switch. If you allow users to download data on floppies, they will need access to the floppy drive; otherwise secure the drive. If you allow users to run their own CDs (checked out from your circulating collection, for example) they will need access to the CD drive.

Consider using keyboards with internal trackballs or free-standing trackball units you can secure to the desktop rather than using free-standing computer mice. Not only are trackballs less subject to theft, they require less desk space to use.

Be aware of the physical security of your building after hours. Banks of PCs set up in front of picture windows are a temptation that thieves may find hard to resist.

PC Startup Protection

When a PC is powered on (or when the reset button is pressed), the processor runs a program called the **BIOS** (Basic Input/Output System). This program and its data are stored on a type of chip called **CMOS** (Complementary Metal Oxide Semiconductor). The information stored here is basic to the operation of the processor. If the BIOS is changed, it is a major problem. The BIOS should never be left unprotected on any library PC, especially a public access PC.

Most PCs support two levels of BIOS passwords: one to access the BIOS configuration and one to run the actual operating system (DOS, Windows 95). PCs do not come with either of these passwords set; you need to do it for each machine. To set these passwords you need to enter the PCs BIOS setup mode.

As the BIOS program starts running, it will display a message as to how to enter the BIOS setup mode. This message will be something to the effect "Press F8 to enter setup." Once you enter setup mode you should set a password. This will prevent patrons from entering setup mode and changing configuration information. Do not forget this password. If you do forget, you will need to open the system case and set certain switches to bypass the password. Your PC documentation discusses this.

While you are in the BIOS, you should also change the boot sequence (the order in which the PC reads data from its drives). The default is drive A first, then drive C. You want to change this to C, then A. This will cause the PC to try to boot first from the internal hard disk rather than the floppy drive and prevents a patron from inserting a floppy and booting the machine, thus by-passing all of your security.

You have the option to set a secondary password (the one required to run the actual operating system). While this is a good security idea, it means that a staff member has to enter this password each time the PC is booted, so most libraries don't set this password.

Operating System

The last thing the BIOS program does is to start up the operating system. The operating system goes through its own startup procedure and completes it by presenting an interface to the user. At this point the user (patron) has complete operator control of the PC. This is not a desirable situation for public access PCs. Patrons could delete files, change parameters that are necessary for the PC to operate, and do all sorts of other undesirable things.

There are numerous ways in which a PC can be protected at this level. Windows 95 itself has built-in protection capabilities using the Policy Editor and Registry. Commercial programs such as Fortres (www.fortres.com) restrict what programs a user can access. Menuing programs such as WinU (www.bardon.com) and Everybody's Menu Builder (www.carl.org) provide restrictions on what programs a user can run and also provide a graphical user interface (different from a Windows 95 desktop) to launch applications (for example, to browse the Internet, access the OPAC, or search CD databases).

Most operating systems provide keyboard shortcuts to access functions in addition to the screen icons. These shortcuts should be disabled; the third party products mentioned can be used to do the disabling.

Applications

The final level of PC security risks lies in the applications themselves. Even if you have secured the PC to the point that it will run only Netscape Navigator or Internet Explorer, the menu options (File, Edit, etc.) inside the launched application are still available to the patron. Would-be hackers can use this as a "back door" to run unauthorized applications.

Some applications are capable of running in a restricted mode to limit user options. However, these are very restrictive and are usually not suitable for public access PCs. The most common third party utility in use today to provide this security inside launched applications is IKIOSK (www.hypertec.com). Using IKIOSK you can choose which options within any application are available to a user. In Netscape Navigator, for example, you can choose to disallow all File options or selectively disallow only certain ones.

Database Security

Most libraries' biggest technology investment is in their library automation system. Thousands of hours and tens or hundreds of thousands of dollars have been invested in building machine readable databases of the library's holdings and patron files. The most frequent answer to the "What do you want to protect?" question is "the library's online database." The most important step in protecting the database is to use a regular backup procedure. Following the vendor's recommended backup schedule and rotating one set of complete backups to an off-site storage location on a regular basis provide the most fundamental protection you can have.

Beyond regular backup procedures, many libraries worry about protecting the database from intruders. This is the most often cited reason for purchasing a firewall. A **firewall** is a barrier placed between your network and the outside world to keep unwanted users from accessing your networked resources. Unfortunately, commercial firewall products are not able to provide the protection libraries seek. Libraries *do* want "outsiders" to access their database; that is the reason online catalogs are on the Web. Commercial firewalls can block access to resources by IP address, but libraries have no way to predict what IP address an Internet-based user might have. Commercial firewalls can restrict access by application, but only to standard IP applications such as Telnet or an HTTP (Web) server. (See the Tech Note on Communications Protocols and TCP/IP Services for more information on standard applications.) Commercial firewalls are not available for proprietary applications such as a library automation vendor's patron input programs or MARC cataloging module.

When library automation systems are running proprietary client software at staff PCs for accessing file maintenance programs, a potential troublemaker needs access to the client software to represent a threat. However, a number of library automation vendors haven't developed a full line of proprietary clients for their systems. Instead, they rely on the standard IP terminal emulation application, Telnet, to connect a networked client PC to the database for staff functions. Even when a vendor has developed specialized clients, those clients often support a "text-based interface" as well, based on Telnet.

A commercial firewall *can* block access from the Internet to Telnet on the library's local system server. However, this means the library can't use Telnet as a way of offering Internet access to its text-based online catalog. If you have your vendor's Web-based online catalog, you can limit Internet users to only the Web view of your catalog, which is why many libraries have decided to offer only the Web OPAC on the Internet.

If you have a Telnet-based catalog available on the Internet, running on the same server as your database and staff applications (which is the most common configuration), a commercial firewall can't help protect your staff functions. You need to rely on staff log ins and passwords, along with the security features your vendor may have developed for its own applications, to protect your database.

If you offer dial-in access for local customers using terminal emulation software over modems, you are offering a character-based protocol connection, not a networked connection. (See the Tech Note on Character/Packet Data for more information.) Your files are as safe as they are from dumb terminals inside your buildings.

Password Administration

Most automated library systems include the option to limit access to various functions by passwords. Using passwords can be a reasonable deterrent to casual troublemakers, but a password is effective only as long as it remains secret. Libraries that never change their passwords, especially in systems where a single password is used by an entire class of employees such as a standard log on for all circulation staff, create an environment that becomes progressively less secure with each personnel change.

An effective password is one that can be remembered by the user but not guessed by anyone else. If you enforce a password scheme that doesn't allow users to select their own passwords, they will write the passwords down, which breaches your security. The best passwords are long and comprised of both numbers and letters. (A password of eight characters would take 3 trillion guesses to break.) Users should never use their own names or the names of their family members, pets, or other interests that are likely to be revealed in the course of casual conversation. Users should be required to change their passwords at regular intervals. The default passwords used on any system should be changed immediately upon installation. Never use system-assigned passwords or examples from system documentation.

Network Security/Firewalls

As libraries expand their networks to include more staff workstations and more publicly accessible resources, security concerns extend beyond just protecting the library's online system. Web servers, CD-ROM servers, and business application servers, such as the library's own internal file server(s), take their place on a network that also includes a connection to the Internet and, maybe, to a city or county government network as well. This is the complex environment in which the answers to the questions "What are you protecting and from whom?" can determine how you design your network(s) and where in that design a firewall can serve your needs.

Complex networks are usually made up of a series of interconnected smaller networks, called **segments** or **subnets.** Firewalls can ensure that not all the segments of a network are equally available to all users. Some segments of an organization's network may be considered the public network, other segments are the private, or intranet, networks. A firewall can sit between the two segments, connected to both the public and private networks and monitoring the

FIGURE 9
Firewall Separating Public and Private Network Segments

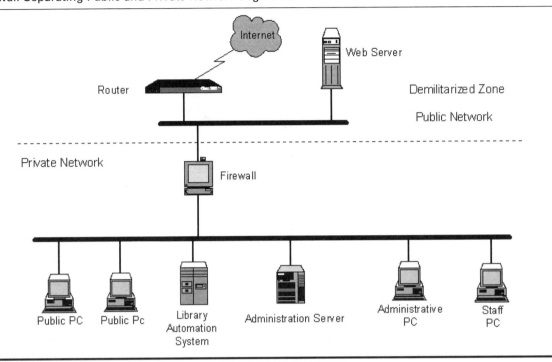

traffic between the two. (See figure 9.) Often the literature of network security will refer to the public network as the "demilitarized zone," a segment of the network that includes servers that are accessible both to users on the internal networks and to users coming from external networks such as the Internet. Libraries are unique in that a library's public network segments are often larger than the internal networks. There are usually more servers you want the public to access than there are servers you want to hide.

A firewall may be a software package you load on a dedicated PC running a standard operating system such as UNIX, Windows NT, or Windows 95, or it may be a "turnkey" combination of hardware and software running under a proprietary operating system. The advantages of the proprietary operating system are that it can be optimized for firewall functions and that it is itself more secure than a commonly used operating system. Basic firewall services are also sometimes included in the software on routers. (See the Network Equipment Definitions Tech Note for more information on routers.)

Firewalls can filter on the basis of the source of an incoming request or on a combination of the requestor's IP address and the IP application requested. Every computer in a TCP/IP network has a unique numeric address (the **IP address**), including computers being used to access the library's resources from the Internet. A firewall can examine the address of an incoming data packet or the address and the IP service requested (Telnet, HTTP, FTP, etc.) and compare that information with a table of permissions that specifies which addresses are allowed which services. If, for example, the library's local system server is behind the firewall and the library does not allow Telnet requests from any computers other than staff computers in its own buildings, only the addresses of the internal computers are put on the "allow" list for Telnet. Any computer with an unauthorized address trying to set up a Telnet session will be denied access. Of course, if Telnet is how Internet users or other libraries get to your online catalog, you can't block access to it. If your online catalog is Telnet based, the firewall will pass all requests through.

This type of filtering is only as good as the tables you put into the firewall. Filtering by address, or by address and IP application, is most often breached because the table of permissions was input improperly or incompletely. If you buy a firewall from a vendor who is responsible for configuring it for you, be sure you can explain who should be able to access what and who should be denied access to what. Then be sure to test the access before you pay the final bill.

Firewalls can also function as **proxy servers.** This means that, instead of permitting a connection to a server behind the firewall, the firewall itself sets up a session with the requestor and a separate session between itself and the target server. It receives requests from the requestor and examines them before it submits the requests to the server. However, to the target server, the request looks as though it is coming from the firewall. The target server never knows there is a requestor on the other side of the firewall. This way, if a hacker tries to take control of the machine she or he is communicating with, it is only the firewall, not the library's database server, that is affected.

Proxy servers work for outgoing connections as well. A computer on an internal segment can use a proxy server to establish an outbound connection with an external resource. The advantage of this type of proxy connection is that the library's internal IP addresses are hidden from view. Your computers are much less vulnerable to attack if their addresses are unknown. Filtering by address can work in reverse, too. A filter table can be used to deny internal users access to specific sites on the Internet, for example.

Designing networks with good security can be complex. They start with secure desktop machines and an implemented password policy. Sometimes they include firewalls. Before you can choose a strategy or select a product, you have to be able to answer the questions "What are we trying to protect?" and "Who are we trying to protect it from?"

Often libraries hire consultants or vendors to install and program some of the elements of their security configuration. Be sure you understand how the products or services meet your "what and who" requirements before you buy and install them. Also be sure, through testing, that the requirements have really been met before you make the final payment.

Additional Resources

Bryan, John. "Build a Firewall." *Byte* 20, no. 4 (Apr. 1995): 91–6.

Dowd, Kevin. *Getting Connected: The Internet at 56K and Up.* Sebastopol, Calif.: O'Reilly & Assoc., 1996.

Farley, Marc. *LAN Times Guide to Security and Data Integrity.* Berkeley, Calif.: Osborne McGraw-Hill, 1996.

Hall, Eric. *Interactive Network Design Manual: Internet Firewall Essentials.* 15 Nov. 1996. Online. Available at http://techweb.cmp.com/nc/netdesign/wall1.html. 19 Nov. 1997.

Lewis, Chris. "Keeping Your Network Safe and Sound." *Network Computing* 8, no. 16 (1 Oct. 1997): 170–5.

The National Computer Security Association certifies firewalls and provides a testing environment for developers' products. Product reviews, testing criteria, and results can be found online.

National Computer Security Association. NSCA FWPD Criteria. Online. Available at http://www.ncsa.com/fpfs/index.html. 19 Nov. 1997.

For a more technical view, see the following:

Cheswick, William R., and Steven M. Bellovin. *Firewalls and Internet Security: Repelling the Wily Hacker.* Reading, Mass.: Addison-Wesley, 1994.

Network Equipment Definitions

When you finish reading this Tech Note, you will be able to

- identify the various hardware components of local and wide area networks

- understand when the components are used and for what purposes

A **local area network** (LAN) connects computers in a work group, department, or building. LANs require data cabling that serves as the medium for message passing between the devices. A **wide area network** (WAN) is a communications system that connects geographically dispersed computers or LANs, usually in two or more separate buildings. A WAN typically uses a telephone connection between sites to serve as the message-passing medium. Every data network, whether a LAN or WAN, is built from one or more components of hardware used to transmit data either between devices on a network or between multiple networks. This network equipment packages data according to the standards supported by the network and transfers it over the wires or airwaves connecting either the devices or the separate networks. The decisions concerning which pieces of equipment are included in a network are made by the network designer based on the connections the network is meant to support.

To understand how network equipment works, it helps to understand the **Open Systems Interconnect** (OSI) seven layer model of networks. Layers 1 through 3 define the packaging and transmission of data. Layers 4 through 7 define the standards for communication between software processes. Layer 1 of network connectivity is the **physical layer.** This set of standards defines how the medium, copper or fiber optic cable, physically transmits electrical or light pulses between devices.

Layer 2, the **datalink layer,** manages the framing of data and the transfer of data to the physical link. *Framing the data* means "packaging the data in a format consistent with the standards of the network in use." Ethernet, Token-Ring, Arcnet, and FDDI (Fiber Distributed Data Interface) networks all have different standards for the frames of data passed by the network. The Medium Access Control (MAC) (see Building Wiring/Data Cabling earlier in the Tech Notes) portion of the datalink layer determines how devices get control of the medium to send data. The datalink layer works with a device's **physical address,** a number unique to each device on a network. The physical address of a device is assigned by the manufacturer of the device.

Layer 3, the **network layer,** establishes, maintains, and disconnects physical and logical connections between two devices. This layer translates **logical addresses,** the address a person would use to describe a server, for example, to physical addresses for transferring data. The distinction between a device's physical address and its logical address is important. Devices that operate at layer 2, the datalink layer, transfer information based on the physical addresses built into each piece of network equipment. Devices that operate at layer 3, the network layer, can identify a destination by its logical address by maintaining tables of data to translate between logical addresses and physical addresses.

Layer 4, the **transport layer,** ensures that data is successfully sent and received between two network devices. If data is lost or damaged in transmission, it is the processes operating at the transport layer that detect the problem and ask for retransmission of the data.

Layer 5, the **session layer,** establishes a communications session between two network devices. It defines, among other things, which device initiates contact, how to reestablish communications if the session is broken, and what synchronization procedures verify data receipt. Layers 4 and 5 of the OSI model often are combined in a single software process.

Layer 6, the **presentation layer**, is responsible for knowing the output and input characteristics of a user's device. Layer 6 makes appropriate translations of data to enable the presentation of that data to the user or to a program.

Layer 7, the **application layer,** defines how applications gain access to network services. This is the level where the user interacts with the network through an application. Hypertext transport protocol (HTTP) and Z39.50 run at layer 7.

Network Interface Card

A **network interface card** (NIC) provides the physical connection to the network. It is typically installed in a card slot in a PC or a server and has a connector that extends from the case of the PC or server where the network data cable can be connected. Because it supports a physical connection, the NIC has to be compatible with the type of data cabling and connectors, or media, used in your network. (See Building Wiring/Data Cabling in previous Tech Note.) If you have a fiber network, you need an NIC with a fiber connector. If your network uses RJ-45 plugs to connect devices, the NIC must have an RJ-45 connector. If your network connection and your NIC are physically dissimilar, a device called a **transceiver** can be used to "translate" between the NIC and the network.

The NIC also has to be compatible with the type of network you are supporting. If you are using an Ethernet network, the NIC also needs to be compatible with your network's speed. Ethernet networks operate at 10 Mbps (10 million bits per second) or 100 Mbps speeds. Many older NICs support only 10 Mbps; more recently developed NICs will support either 10 Mbps or 100 Mbps. A third standard, Gigabit Ethernet, operating at 1,000 Mbps, is in development. Although Gigabit Ethernet may be used for servers and other devices connected to a network, it is unlikely to become widely used for desktop machines any time soon.

Terminal Server

Libraries that want to continue using character-based terminals in a networked environment need some way to translate the serial data produced by terminals into the packets of data transferred by networks and back again. The device that provides this service is called a **terminal server.** One side of a terminal server has connections that can be used to plug terminals into the device. The other side of the device has a place to plug in a network data cable. This network connection is to a network interface inside the terminal server. Just as with network interface cards for PCs and servers, the network connection in the terminal server must be compatible with the particular network protocol you are using, with the network's speed, and with the physical medium—copper data cable or optical fiber. (Again, refer to the Building Wiring/Data Cabling section of Tech Notes for additional information on cabling.)

Terminal servers can also be used with modems to provide terminal emulation dial-in access to a library's catalog. If your online catalog is available to dial-in users via a terminal emulation program on the user's PC, a terminal server with modems instead of terminals connected to it can be used to support dial-in service.

Hub/Concentrator

Every PC in a LAN must be connected to a server or to the other PCs to pass data between the devices. However, each server or PC has only one network connection on its network interface card. A **wiring hub,** also sometimes called a **wiring concentrator,** makes it possible for each device to connect to multiple other devices. Although there are some LAN designs in which cabling is strung from device to device, it is more common to run data cable from each device back to a central point, often called the **wiring closet,** where a hub is located. Each device's data cable plugs into a connector on the hub, which establishes a physical connection to every other device connected to that hub. It is also possible to link multiple hubs together, thereby linking the devices attached to each hub to the devices on all the linked hubs. (See figure 10.)

FIGURE 10
Multiple Hub Network

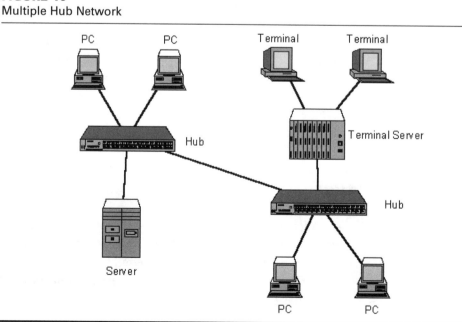

The types of application servers, devices that can be linked together using a hub, include but are not limited to file servers, PCs, terminal servers, print servers (special devices that manage networked printers), and CD servers. Again, the devices and the hubs have to be compatible in protocol, speed, and media. Hubs will often have two or more types of physical medium connections, one to connect with desktop devices, another to connect with another hub or server.

If a single hub connects a server to all the devices in a network, it is sometimes referred to as a **collapsed backbone.** Hubs can also be **intelligent,** which means they have the ability to be managed remotely from a centralized location rather than requiring a staff member or technician to go on-site to troubleshoot problems. Intelligent hubs can also trap and report statistics about their usage if a library has a network management software package that can analyze the data. Intelligent hubs or hubs that can be upgraded to include remote management are more expensive than plain hubs.

Bridge

In an Ethernet network, every data packet that a device puts on the wire is broadcast to every other device; the device to which it is addressed is the only one that captures the packet, however. The other devices in the network see the broadcast, but they do not respond because the packet is not addressed to them. As networks grow, this broadcast traffic can get quite heavy, slowing down the entire network. Often, to relieve the response-time problems, a single network will be broken into two or more smaller networks. However, these smaller networks may occasionally need to share data. A **bridge** is a device that connects two similar networks, taking data packets from one network and putting them on another network as required. (See figure 11.)

FIGURE 11
Similar Networks Connected by a Bridge

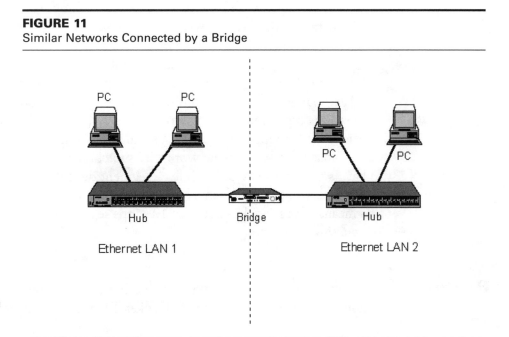

A bridge examines the physical address (layer 2 of the OSI model) to which a packet is bound and makes a decision about whether the device is located on the network where the packet is traveling. If a packet from device 1 on LAN A is bound for device 2 on LAN B, the bridge will pass it from LAN A to LAN B. If the packet from device 1 on LAN A is addressed to device 2 on LAN A, the bridge does not pass it to LAN B. This ensures that the broadcasts of each LAN are seen by the other LAN only when it is necessary to complete the connection between two devices.

Bridges determine where the devices are by analyzing traffic on their connected LANs and storing information about which device is available through each of the bridge's connections.

In addition to reducing network traffic, bridges can also be used to connect networks that are built on different physical media, for example, a fiber-based Ethernet network and a copper wire-based Ethernet network, or to connect two physically separate LANs over telephone lines. However, the networks must be the same; that is, they must both be Ethernet or both be Token Ring. Bridges do not change the frame structure of the packets they transfer. Many integrated library system vendors' first implementations of wide area networking were based on bridging data between branches and the library's computer central site. Bridges are less common today, but they still are useful in some environments.

Switch

A switching hub, also known as an **Ethernet switch,** is a device that reduces traffic on a LAN through microsegmentation, or breaking the LAN up into multiple segments with very few devices per segment. Switches are sophisticated bridges. As electrical circuit technology evolved, the capacity of bridges to handle multiple LANs grew. The new "switching" circuitry resulted in the new name for the devices.

In a switched network there may be only one or two users on a segment. The switching hub examines the destination address of packets coming in from one of its segments and passes those packets through to the segment on which that address is located. Essentially, the hub performs like a bridge between the segments of the network connected to it. Switching hubs were developed when applications such as multimedia applications began to flood the capacity of 10 Mbps networks. By switching the segments, each segment has its own pathway to the hub; a segment doesn't see the broadcast traffic of devices on other segments of the network. Switches are sometimes used as a means of passing data between 10 Mbps segments and 100 Mbps segments on a single network.

Router

A router is a device that traditionally has been used to connect dissimilar LANs. For example, Ethernet LANs and Token-Ring LANs can only communicate

FIGURE 12
Dissimilar Networks Connected by a Router

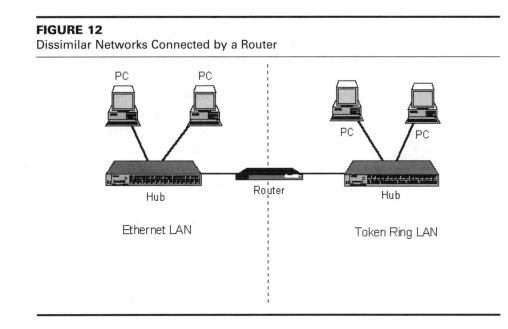

through a router. This is because the router, which works at layer 3 of the OSI model, is capable of repackaging frames of data, for example, Ethernet formatted data into Token-Ring formatted data. This means a router can receive a data packet framed for Ethernet from one of its network connections, rebuild it as a Token-Ring frame, and send the rebuilt frame out over another of the router's network connections. (See figure 12.)

As networks grew and became more complex, especially as wide area networks were developed, routers were often used to connect remote LANs of the same type as well. (See figure 13.) Routers can pass packets based on logical addresses rather than physical addresses and provide traffic control when more than one pathway exists between two end points. The Internet is such an environment, and routers are used to move data to and through the Internet.

FIGURE 13
Wide Area Network

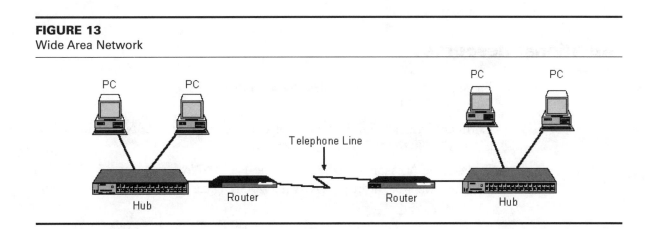

Because routers have many more capabilities than bridges, they are more complex to set up and more challenging to troubleshoot when problems develop. Most libraries let their vendors handle the programming of their routers. The library defines what type of data needs to flow where, and the supplier of the router builds the **routing tables** that actually determine the flow of data between networks and routers. When a router receives a packet of data, it looks at the destination address of the packet, then checks the routing tables to determine where to send the packet next. These routing tables can be static, programmed once and expected to remain the same, or dynamic, built and continuously validated by special routing protocol software. Since libraries generally have stable wide area network connections between their branches and their Internet service providers, static routing is most often used in libraries. This means that changing the wide area network in any way will probably require reprogramming a library's routers; therefore, any changes in the wide area network should involve the library's router supplier.

CSU/DSU

Channel service units (CSUs) and **data service units** (DSUs) are two separate devices that are usually combined into a single box and are often treated as one device. A CSU connects to a digital telephone line and provides diagnostic and testing functions for the phone company supplying the line. A DSU translates digital data coming from a network device, such as a router, a bridge, or a multiplexer, into the type of electrical signals used by the phone system. (See Telecommunications Options in Tech Notes for more on CSU/DSUs.)

Multiplexers

Multiplexers are pieces of network equipment that can transmit only serial data, not the packet data of the Internet. Many libraries have multiplexers installed because they were the standard way to transmit data between branches and a centrally located computer in integrated library systems in the 1980s and early 1990s.

Additional Resources

Breyer, Robert, and Sean Riley. *Switched and Fast Ethernet.* 2d ed. Emeryville, Calif.: Ziff-Davis, 1996.

Corrigan, Patrick. "Fundamentals of Network Design." *LAN* 12, no. 2 (Feb. 1997): 93–6.

Fogle, Dave. "Lesson 90: Ethernet Frame Types." *Network Magazine.* 1996. Online. Available at http://www.networkmagazine.com/tutors/9602tut.htm. 4 Feb. 1998.

LAN Tutorial: A Complete Introduction to Local Area Networks. 3d ed. San Francisco: Miller Freeman, 1996.

Nunemacher, Greg. *LAN Primer.* 3d ed. New York: M&T, 1995.

Schatt, Stan. *Understanding Local Area Networks.* 4th ed. Indianapolis: Sams, 1993.

Sheldon, Tom. *LAN Times Encyclopedia of Networking.* Berkeley, Calif.: Osborne McGraw-Hill, 1994.

Shnier, Mitchell. *Dictionary of PC Hardware and Data Communications Terms.* Sebastopol, Calif.: O'Reilly & Assoc., 1996.

Steinke, Steve. "Lesson 92: Getting Data Over the Telephone Line." *Network Magazine.* 1996. Online. Available at http://www.networkmagazine.com/tutors/9604tut.htm. 4 Feb. 1998.

———. "Lesson 105: Switching vs. Routing." *Network* 12, no. 5 (May 1997): 27–8.

For a more technical view, see the following:

Baker, Fred. "How Do Routers Work." *LAN* 12, no. 3 (Mar. 1997): 87–91.

"Routing toward the Future." *InfoWorld* 19 (8 Sept. 1997): 73–82.

Network Operating Systems

When you finish reading this Tech Note, you will be able to

- describe the function of a network operating system

- identify the most widely used available network operating systems

An **operating system** is software on a computer that gives application software access to the hardware of the computer. If an application needs to read data from a disk drive or send a report to a printer, it is the operating system that makes it possible. Most operating systems were developed to provide the interface between one computer and its applications. In addition to managing its applications, a server on a network also needs to manage its communications with multiple clients. Sometimes a networked application may need to access multiple computers to operate. Therefore, special operating systems—network operating systems—were developed to run on networks.

There are usually at least two operating systems in most networks, the operating system of the client machines and the operating system of the server(s). Client machines typically run a standard desktop operating system such as Windows 95 (98, etc.), OS/2, Windows NT Workstation, or Mac OS. Each of these client operating systems has built-in communications features that allow these machines to participate in a network.

Servers usually run an operating system specially designed to maximize their efficiency in a high demand, multiuser environment. The operating systems most commonly used for servers in libraries include Novell's NetWare, Microsoft's NT Server, and several varieties of UNIX, including Sun's Solaris.

UNIX

UNIX was one of the earliest multiuser operating systems to support networking. Developed in the 1960s, it enjoyed a surge of popularity on college and university campuses in the 1980s as networks first became generally available. It was also adopted as a U.S. federal government standard in the 1980s. Many library integrated system vendors either developed their applications to run under UNIX or migrated their existing applications to operate under UNIX in the 1980s; therefore, many public libraries installed UNIX systems in the 1980s and 1990s. TCP/IP, the communications protocol of the Internet, is the native communications protocol of the UNIX operating system. (See the Tech Note on Communications Protocols and TCP/IP Services for more information on TCP/IP.)

Although UNIX works well with the library applications developed for it, it remains a very challenging operating system to manage. Unlike network operating systems developed in the 1980s and 1990s that usually have graphical user interfaces or menus to help in configuring and operating the network, UNIX systems generally rely on cryptic commands from the operator. Although many library system administrators have mastered the arcane requirements of UNIX, most library vendors have written special user interfaces to make their UNIX systems easier to operate. While this helps with the administration of a library's integrated system, it doesn't address the problems a library faces if it tries to add a native UNIX machine to its network to support other services, such as a Web or e-mail server. As a result, UNIX has not been widely adopted by libraries as a general-purpose network operating system unless the library has UNIX expertise on staff.

Novell's NetWare

NetWare, a network operating system developed by Novell, was the first operating system designed specifically to share resources such as files and printers among PCs. NetWare required users to load special software on client machines that intercepted a user's command to open a file or print a document and redirected that command to a file and print server on the network. NetWare's target market was businesses that needed to share files, so it showed up first in libraries in the business office. As CD-ROMs became popular, third-party software developers built applications designed to share access to CD-ROMs on top of NetWare. Library software developers who had written PC-based circulation and online catalog systems often adopted NetWare as a way to provide multiuser access to their software as well. As the number of library uses for NetWare increased, so did the number of installations. Many libraries also found their parent agencies, city and county governments, adopting NetWare as an agency standard. This sometimes caused a problem when the library wanted to buy a UNIX-based integrated system.

The biggest drawback of NetWare from a library's perspective is the system's proprietary communications protocol. When NetWare was developed in the 1980s, the Internet was still primarily a research network, not the public communications medium it is today. Novell developed its own communications protocol, IPX/SPX, to communicate between devices on the network. Although Novell has since incorporated TCP/IP into new releases of NetWare, many of the legacy NetWare systems, at release 3.x of the software, are still limited to IPX/SPX communications. This makes them challenging to integrate into a library's network design if the library's primary network objective is accessing Internet resources.

Windows NT

Microsoft's entry in network operating systems is NT Server. Microsoft spent so many years ensuring its domination at the desktop level that it came to the world of network operating systems somewhat late. Some network gurus would say that NT Server is still not as good a network operating system as the others. However, Microsoft is a dominant market force, and many library vendors are betting that NT Server will be the premier network operating system of the early twenty-first century. Many integrated system vendors who built systems to run under UNIX or migrated their systems to UNIX in the 1980s are now building new systems or migrating their existing systems to operate under NT Server. Other vendors who are writing new networked applications for libraries, such as interlibrary loan software, are developing their applications to run under NT from the start.

Other Network Operating Systems

Several other network operating systems are installed in libraries. These include System, Inc.'s Banyan Vines and Artisoft's LANtastic. Both were developed about the same time as NetWare; neither achieved the market penetration and widespread adoption of the Novell operating system. LANtastic began as a peer-to-peer operating system, not as a client server.

IBM offers a network operating system as well, OS/2 Warp. Although it is highly regarded by those who use it, there is relatively little software that runs on it. It has not made significant inroads into the library marketplace.

As libraries' use of technology goes well beyond the offerings of integrated system vendors to include Web servers, CD-ROM servers, e-mail servers, firewalls, and Z39.50 gateways (see the last section of Tech Notes), they are reaching into the world of commercial software not built exclusively for libraries. Much of that commercial software is being developed to run under NT Server, which is particularly good at running applications on a network. This contrasts with NetWare, which is optimized to share access to files. Although libraries do some file sharing among staff over their networks, their primary use of networked servers is to provide access to multiple applications. As a result, more and more libraries are looking to NT as the network operating system of choice.

Additional Resources

"Banyan Enhances Its Network OS." *InfoWorld* 18, no. 51–52 (22 Dec. 1997): 43.

Machrone, Bill. "Kind Words for Novell—For a Change." *PC Week* 14, no. 52 (15 Dec. 1997): 81.

Nunemacher, Greg. *LAN Primer*. 3d ed. New York: M&T, 1995.

Orfali, Robert, Dan Harkey, and Jeri Edwards. *The Essential Client/Server Survival Guide*. 2d ed. New York: Wiley, 1996.

Schatt, Stan. *Understanding Local Area Networks*. 4th ed. Indianapolis: Sams, 1993.

Surkan, Michael. "The Changing NOS Landscape: Network Operating System Is Covering New Ground." *PC Week* 14, no. 42 (6 Oct. 1997): 125.

———. "Feature Creep Redefines and Expands NOSes." *PC Week* 14, no. 47 (10 Nov. 1997). Online. Available at http://www.zdnet.com/pcweek/reviews/1110/10nos.html. 3 Oct. 1998.

———. "Internet Forces a United Front in NOS Territory." *PC Week* 14, no. 42 (6 Oct. 1997): 125.

———. "SUN Warms Solaris." *PC Week* 14, no. 38 (8 Sept. 1997): 95.

Telecommunications Options

When you finish reading this Tech Note, you will be able to

- define basic telecommunications terms

- understand the differences between available telecommunications services

Telephone deregulation in the 1980s created new competitive opportunities for companies that wanted to offer telephone services or to develop telephone equipment. Although it took some time to develop, the results of deregulation are the multitude of phone services available today. Further competition, spurred by the Telecommunications Act of 1996, is bringing even more potential suppliers into the market and continuing to expand the options for transmitting voice and data. That is the good news; the bad news is that somehow you have to understand enough about the options to choose one that will meet your needs at a competitive cost. Once you have made that decision, you need to revisit it at least biannually to confirm that it is still the best choice. Services are cropping up so fast, and telecommunications tariffs are being changed so frequently, that it could be cost effective to change your telecommunications configuration every three to four years.

Basic Terms

Switches

A **switch** is an electrical or mechanical device that opens and closes connections. If your telephone switch is located on your premises it is called a **PBX,** or private branch exchange. If you use a Centrex system, or plain old telephone service (POTS), the switch is phone company equipment located in the phone company's central office, or **CO.** COs are also called *switching stations* and are usually located throughout the community. Different switches can support different types of phone company services, which is why some services are not available in some areas. Switch-to-switch communication is how phone companies route calls between two users. One of the major growth and development areas in the era of deregulation is in phone company switches.

Copper wire or fiber optic cable runs from the phone service termination point in your building to the nearest CO's switch. The COs are connected to each other to pass traffic between them. The national network of telecommunications is based on connections between phone company switches.

Analog/Digital Service

One distinguishing characteristic of phone services is whether they are analog or digital. **Analog lines,** developed to transmit voices, are set up to pass electrical representations of sound waves from the user's telephone to the phone company switch. Data streams coming from computing devices don't produce sound waves, they produce electrical pulses that are the equivalent of bits of data. This is why computers need modems to connect with voice phone lines. Modems turn the electrical pulses coming from the computer into sound waves so the switch will recognize them and know how to handle them when they arrive. **Digital services** do not expect sound waves from the user; they expect the electrical pulses of data. Ironically, whether the signal leaves the user in analog or digital format, once it arrives at the phone company's switch it becomes digital because all of the connections between phone company switches are digital connections.

The only exception to this is in the many private telephone companies that still serve isolated areas throughout the country. Sometimes these telephone companies are still using analog switches. The signals from these companies may not be digitized until they are received by the regional telephone operating company in the area.

Packet/Circuit Service

Phone services can either pass packets of data or streams of data. (See the Character/Packet Data section in Tech Notes.) In **packet services,** the data is contained in discrete packages, each of which is addressed to a specific destination. The data goes from the originator to the local phone company switch; from there it is routed through a series of phone company switches until it gets to its destination. How the data moves through the phone company switches is irrelevant to the user as long as it gets where it is going. Messages large enough to be broken into multiple packets can even be routed different ways through the maze of phone switches; special information in the address ensures that it is put back together in sequence when it is delivered.

Streams of data can also move from user to destination through a predetermined electrical path called a **circuit.** In **circuit service,** the phone switches set up a direct connection between the call originator and the call destination; the data can then be transmitted without special destination addressing because it can only go one place—to the connected destination. Circuits can either be switched or nonswitched. A **switched circuit** is one that is set up on demand. When you pick up your phone to make a voice call, you are requesting a switched circuit between your number and the number you are calling. At the end of the call that circuit is dismantled. **Nonswitched circuits** are permanent connections between two points; you can't "switch" to another destination.

Line Speed or Bandwidth

The amount of data transmission capacity a telephone line has is called its speed or **bandwidth.** A single voice-grade telephone circuit can transmit a maximum of 64,000 bits of data per second (64 Kbps), regardless of whether that data represents an analog sound wave or bits of computer data. The phone company usually uses 8,000 of those bits for its own purposes, to pass information on the status of the line, for example. So the user actually has access to 56,000 bits of transmission capacity every second. This transmission capacity is often referred to as a **56K line,** although occasionally you will see them called **DS0 lines.**

To enhance their use of the copper wire running between a customer's premises and the CO, the phone companies can combine 24 circuits on a pair of wires using a sharing technique called multiplexing. When 24 lines of 64,000 bits each are combined together, they have 1,544,000 bits per second (1.544 Mbps) of transmission capacity. This is called a **T1** or a **DS1 line.** Again, the phone company usually reserves some of that capacity for its own signaling, so the customer typically has access to 1.536 Mbps. It is possible in some areas to buy only a portion of the 24 circuits in a T1 line. These lines are called **FT1,** or fractional T1 lines.

T3 or **DS3 lines** have the capacity of 28 T1s (44.736 Mbps). This means a library using a T3 line is buying phone capacity that the company could have sold to 672 individual subscribers, which helps explain why T3 lines are so expensive.

Point-to-Point Lines

Most library phone lines installed in the 1970s and 1980s to connect branches to a centrally located integrated library system were nonswitched circuits, also called point-to-point lines or **leased lines.** These lines connect only two points; therefore, the data between those points can be passed without any address information. It also means that only the two end points use the line; no one else shares the transmission capacity of the line. If you buy a 56K line, you get the full 56 K capacity, but no more. The costs of point-to-point lines are generally related to the distance between the two sites.

Point-to-point lines can be either analog or digital lines. If the line is analog, the computer equipment on it is connected to the line by a modem. If the line is digital, the computer equipment is connected to the line by a channel service unit/data service unit (CSU/DSU). The speed of a point-to-point line is dictated by the transmission capacity of the modem or the CSU/DSU. If you have 19.2 Kbps modems connected to the line, data will be transmitted at 19,200 bits per second (Kbps) regardless of the fact that the line has the capacity to transmit at 56 Kbps.

Frame Relay

Frame relay is a service that often replaces point-to-point lines. Frame relay is a packet-based service, which means that each package of data being sent includes its origination and destination addresses. This identification of each packet gives the phone company some additional options for installing phone lines that can lead to a reduction in cost for the user.

The typical multibranch library wide area network is a hub-and-spoke arrangement. Each branch has a phone line that terminates at the central library or the computer center where the integrated system is housed. In a point-to-point network, the central library has an incoming phone line for each branch.

FIGURE 14
Point-to-Point Wide Area Network

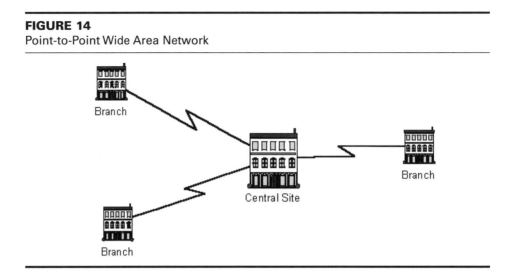

(See figure 14.) In a frame relay network the phone company groups all of the incoming packets from all of the branches together and sends them to the central site over a single phone line. (See figure 15.) It also splits out packets from the central site and sends them back over the individual branch lines. It does this through switch-based software that sets up **permanent virtual circuits** (PVCs) between the branches and the central site.

Because all of this grouping and splitting goes on inside phone company switches, the cost of a frame relay line is based on the distance between the origination site and its nearest CO instead of the distance between the origination and destination points. The only exception is when the phone company doesn't have frame relay switches in all of its COs. In that case, you

FIGURE 15
Frame Relay Wide Area Network

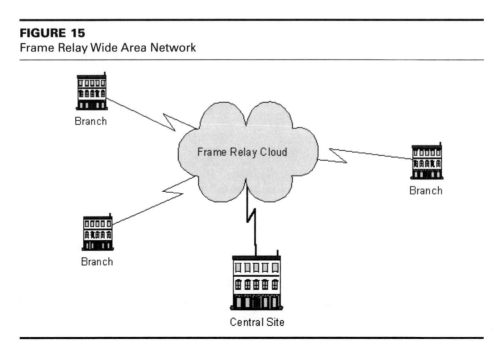

might find yourself paying **backhaul charges,** which are the distance-based charges from your origination point to the nearest frame relay switch. In some locations the backhaul charges are so high that they make point-to-point lines the less expensive of the two options.

The network equipment needed to support a single frame relay line at the central library is usually less expensive than equipment needed to support multiple point-to-point lines. The equipment in a branch is usually about the same cost for both services.

Integrated Services Digital Network (ISDN)

ISDN is a switched digital service. That means you can use an ISDN line to connect to multiple destinations, much like your voice phone. ISDN can transmit both voice and data; voice transmission is possible because ISDN telephones translate voice sound waves to digital bits before they put the data on the wire headed for the phone switch.

ISDN lines are available in two bandwidths. An ISDN **basic rate interface** (BRI) line has the capacity to transmit 128 Kbps of data over two channels. It is like linking two 56/64K lines together. With ISDN the user can use one channel for voice and one for data, both channels can be used for data, or each channel can be set up to support a separate voice line. Most libraries using ISDN are using both channels for data transmission.

An ISDN **primary rate interface** (PRI) line is the equivalent of a T1 line; it has 24 channels at 64 Kbps each. One channel is used to manage the line, so the user has access to 23 channels of transmission capacity. These channels can be treated as 23 separate lines or grouped together to provide higher bandwidth.

ISDN requires a call setup each time a connection is initiated. This is the equivalent of dialing a phone number to make a phone call, but it happens much faster in ISDN. The ISDN connection is set up by software in your network's communication equipment and dismantled when it is no longer in use. If you are using ISDN for data transmission, the destination you are calling must be supporting ISDN as well.

ISDN has not been widely used in libraries because of the costs. In many states, ISDN charges are based on a per-connection fee: each time your ISDN equipment sets up a call, there is a charge. Often there is a per-minute charge for connect time as well. To budget effectively, libraries have to assume they will be connected all the hours they are open, so the connection costs and per-minute fees are often more expensive than a point-to-point or frame relay 56 Kbps line. Recently, however, to promote the use of ISDN, some phone companies have been offering flat-rate monthly charges for ISDN services with no usage-based costs. Under these circumstances, many libraries are finding that ISDN is a cost-effective way to increase bandwidth for branches that have been using a 56 Kbps line and that don't need the capacity of a full T1.

Switched Multimegabit Data Service (SMDS)

SMDS is a switched digital service based on transmitting cells of data of the same size. This contrasts with packets of data that can vary widely in size. SMDS services are not widely available and are usually limited to metropolitan areas. Because SMDS is a switched service, its cost is usually based on connection time, giving it the same cost disadvantages for a library that were described under ISDN.

SMDS has some technical advantages over phone lines in delivering video and audio data, but many of those advantages are being offset by the continuing development of frame relay. For a library, SMDS will work as well in transferring data between a central site and branches as frame relay or ISDN. It doesn't have any particular advantages or disadvantages, so cost and SMDS availability in the site(s) you want to connect to are usually the determining factors in selecting SMDS or one of the other available services.

Asymmetrical Digital Subscriber Line (ADSL)

ADSL is a newly emerging technology that makes it possible for phone companies to deliver high bandwidth service over the existing copper wires that are in most people's homes. The asymmetrical part is that the **downstream bandwidth,** what you receive, is much larger than the **upstream bandwidth,** what you can send. How much bandwidth is available is a function of how far the user is from a CO. If you are within two miles of a CO, you could get speeds of up to 9 million bits per second downstream and 640,000 bits per second upstream. At four miles, you can get the equivalent of T1 downstream capacity.

ADSL is not widely available in 1998 as this is written. Compaq, Microsoft, Intel, the regional Bell operating companies, and GTE recently joined together to further the development of the technology and quicken its adoption. It is a technology that bears watching for libraries, particularly libraries that use dial-up accounts to access the Internet.

Cable Service

Cable television companies have wires or fiber into nearly 60 million American homes and some government offices and are looking for ways to expand the use of that infrastructure. One obvious opportunity is data transmission. The growing demand for high bandwidth Internet access, coupled with development of new generations of cable modems, has fueled the cable companies' move into providing data along with television signals.

Cable company installations were originally built on copper coaxial cable. In the last several years cable companies have begun replacing that copper with fiber cable. Cable modems developed to operate with the newer fiber installations have full, two-way transmission capacity. Copper-based data transmission is download only, and it requires the addition of a dial-up connection from a conventional modem to complete the two-way connection.

Cable transmission is typically asymmetrical, which means that the downstream capacity of the link (for the data you receive) is larger than the upstream capacity (for data you send). Cable connections are also shared connections: the subscribers on each cable segment share the data transfer capacity of that segment, and all the segments together share the cable company's connection to the Internet. This means the actual performance of a cable connection is dependent on the number of other users sharing that segment and the amount of use they make of it. Cable companies need experience with data to determine what is the optimum load of subscribers per segment to ensure adequate performance.

Some libraries are using cable providers to access the Internet. The important things to keep in mind when considering cable are the types of use you intend to make of the cable, the Internet services you will expect from your Internet service provider, and the maintenance support you will receive from your cable company.

If you are using the cable system just to access the Internet from staff or public PCs, the asymmetrical nature of cable data is appropriate for your usage. However, if you intend to support a server on your cable connection (your online catalog or library Web server, for example), the cable company must understand that the server will have a higher upstream requirement than a typical user. A server delivers far more data than it receives, which is the opposite usage pattern from that of a typical client.

Many libraries also rely on their Internet service provider for services such as electronic mail boxes or hosting library Web pages. Cable companies can certainly offer these services, but be sure to ask about these services if you need them. This will be particularly important if your local cable company is planning to start their foray into data delivery by offering service to the library. If the cable company isn't offering these services and you need them, you will have to make arrangements with other companies to provide them.

Ask, too, about the service and support the cable company intends to offer. What is the priority of reestablishing service in the event of an outage? Segments to television subscriber homes are usually repaired immediately, even on nights and weekends. Will a segment that is used primarily for data, as the library's connection will be, receive the same priority service? If so, get in it your contract.

Wireless Transmission

There are two types of wireless transmission in use today: radio frequency and microwave. Although neither provides the bandwidth of a local area network (typically 10 million bits per second), either can offer a faster speed than a T1 line if the conditions for data transmission are met. Both use the airwaves to transmit data, which makes them less expensive on a monthly basis than a phone line. However, until June 1997, there weren't any adopted standards for wireless network transmissions, which slowed the adoption of wireless technology. Even with the agreement to the first standard, there are still a lot of questions to be answered and development to be done before wireless transmission will be as common as phone-based services.

Microwave

Microwave is typically used for long distance communications. It operates over a specific piece of the electromagnetic spectrum, licensed by the FCC. Each microwave user is licensed to operate at one frequency and no other. This means that if you want to use microwave for data transmission, you need to get an FCC license or share another agency's preexisting license.

Microwave transmissions are **line-of-sight transmissions.** This means there must be an unobstructed view between two microwave transmitters for them to exchange signals. Mountains, trees, tall buildings, even heavy rain, can all obstruct microwave transmissions. The transmitters need to be relatively close together as well, typically within 12 miles of each other.

Microwave equipment is expensive. Although freedom from monthly charges can offset the initial purchase and installation price of microwave equipment in large networks, for small installations the costs can be prohibitive.

Finally, microwave is not a technology supported by Internet service providers or any of the traditional library automation vendors. A library seeking to base its communications on microwave will either need to install and manage its own microwave equipment or seek the assistance of another agency with microwave expertise for configuration and support.

Spread Spectrum Radio Frequency

Spread spectrum technologies operate in the unregulated portion of the electromagnetic spectrum; no FCC license is required. Spread spectrum has a longer distance range than microwave, potentially as far as 20 to 25 miles. Because it operates in the unregulated portion of the spectrum, spread spectrum data transmissions compete with other radio frequency uses for access to the airwaves. Congested cities with lots of radio traffic can often result in a very short effective range for spread spectrum transmissions.

As with microwave, spread spectrum is not supported by most library suppliers, so any library intending to use a spread spectrum network will need to identify its own configuration and support people.

Cellular Telephone

Cellular telephone service is sometimes used to connect bookmobiles with a centrally located computer or the Internet. This requires two phone lines: a cellular line for the bookmobile and a regular line at the central site. A cellular modem is needed on the bookmobile and a modem optimized for receiving cellular traffic is recommended at the central site. Cellular minutes can be quite costly. Although progress has been made in recent years, some of the same transmission problems as those of microwaves exist.

Additional Resources

Bezar, David. *LAN Times Guide to Telephony.* Berkeley, Calif.: Osborne McGraw-Hill, 1995.

Breyer, Robert, and Sean Riley. *Switched and Fast Ethernet.* 2d ed. Emeryville, Calif.: Ziff-Davis, 1996.

Conover, Joel. "Bridging the Miles with 10-Mbps Spread Spectrum Wireless Networking." *Network Computing* 8, no. 20 (1 Nov. 1997): 144–8.

Corrigan, Patrick. "Fundamentals of Network Design." *LAN* 12, no. 2 (Feb. 1997): 93–6.

Fogle, Dave. "Lesson 90: Ethernet Frame Types." *Network Magazine.* Feb. 1996. Online. Available at http://www.networkmagazine.com/tutors/9602tut.htm. 4 Feb. 1998.

Freed, Les. "Faster Connections." *PC Magazine Online.* 10 Feb. 1998. Online. Available at http://www.zdnet.com/pcmag/pclabs/nettools/1703/tools.htm. 3 Oct. 1998.

Held, Gilbert. "Shopping for Frame Relay." *Network* 12, no. 13 (Dec. 1997): 83–7.

Henderson, Tom. "I Shot the Tariff." *LAN* 11, no. 2 (Feb. 1996): 101–4.

Hurwicz, Mike. "In Search of the Ideal WAN." *LAN* 12, no. 1 (Jan. 1997): 99–102.

———. "On-Line from a LAN." *LAN* 11, no. 5 (May 1996): 85–90.

Karve, Anita. "The Wide World of Wireless." *Network* 12, no. 3 (Dec. 1997): 42–8.

Krivda, Cheryl D. "Frame Relay Comes of Age." *LAN* 11, no. 12 (Nov. 1996): 117–24.

LAN Tutorial: A Complete Introduction to Local Area Networks. 3d ed. San Francisco: Miller Freeman, 1996.

Newman, Jeff. "Avoid WAN Outages: Three Leased Line Failover Devices to Keep You Connected." *Network Computing* 8, no. 12 (15 Nov. 1997): 136–7.

Nunemacher, Greg. *LAN Primer.* 3d ed. New York: M&T, 1995.

Schatt, Stan. *Understanding Local Area Networks.* 4th ed. Indianapolis: Sams, 1993.

Sheldon, Tom. *LAN Times Encyclopedia of Networking.* Berkeley, Calif.: Osborne McGraw-Hill, 1994.

Shnier, Mitchell. *Dictionary of PC Hardware and Data Communications Terms.* Sebastopol, Calif.: O'Reilly & Assoc., 1996.

Steinke, Steve. "Lesson 92: Getting Data over the Telephone Line." *Network Magazine.* 1996. Online. Available at http://www.networkmagazine.com/tutors/9604tut.htm. 4 Feb. 1998.

————. "Lesson 105: Switching vs. Routing." *Network* 12, no. 5 (May 1997): 27–8.

————. "Rehab for Copper Wire." *LAN* 12, no. 2 (Feb. 1997): 57–62.

————. "Tutorial 89: Basic Phone Services and Circuits." *LAN* 11, no. 1 (Jan. 1996): 27–8.

"Wireless Networking." *InfoWorld.* 3 Nov. 1997. Online. Available at http://www.infoworld.com/cgi-bin/displayArchive.pl?/97/44/wirelesa.dat.htm. 3 Oct. 1998.

Weil, Nancy. "Cable-Modem Security Issues Come to the Fore." *InfoWorld* 19, no. 45 (10 Nov. 1997): 77.

Wu, Daniel. "Client-Server over Frame Relay." *Network* 12, no. 10 (Oct. 1997): 105–9.

For a more technical view, see the following:

Baker, Fred. "How Do Routers Work." *LAN* 12, no. 3 (Mar. 1997): 87–91.

"Routing toward the Future." *InfoWorld* 19 (8 Sept. 1997): 73–82.

Z39.50

When you finish reading this Tech Note, you will be able to

- explain Z39.50 and its role in library automation

- understand where to purchase Z39.50 functionality

- determine if Z39.50 is important to your organization's technology planning

Z39.50 is the American National Standards Institute's *Information Retrieval Service Definition and Protocol Specifications for Library Applications*. This means that the American National Standards Institute (ANSI) has published a standard that defines how two computers can communicate with each other for the purposes of one computer retrieving information from the other. With Z39.50, the *how* of the communication is defined, not what type of information can be retrieved. That distinction is an important one.

Although Z39.50 is generally thought of in the library world as a way to retrieve bibliographic data, the standard was not intended to be limited to just bibliographic data. It is an information-retrieval standard and, indeed, after years of being used primarily as a way to retrieve online catalog records from different integrated library systems, there are now systems available to be searched using Z39.50 clients that are not bibliographic systems at all. The U.S. government, for example, is using the Z39.50 standard as the basis for its Government Information Locator System (GILS), and museums are experimenting with it in a project on the computer exchange of museum information. Solinet has tested it as a way to retrieve information from community information files. Additional tests and experiments are developing in libraries and in other industries as well.

The Z39.50 standard existed for several years before it was actually implemented. The first serious implementation of the standard was developed in the early 1990s to make it possible for the users of one integrated vendor's online catalog to search the database of another vendor's online catalog. Based on the experience of trying to make version 1 of the Z39.50 standard work in a real world application, version 2 was drafted and adopted in 1992. Version 2 is the form of the Z39.50 standard most library vendors initially adopted. Some, but not all, vendors incorporated some of the features of version 3 when it was approved in 1995. The primary difference between versions 2 and 3, from a public library's perspective, is that version 3 included the transfer of status information from a Z39.50 server to a Z39.50 client. This meant that the standard not only supported finding out if another library had the title in its catalog, it also let the user know if a copy of that title was available for loan.

As it has been implemented to date, Z39.50 is designed as a network application. The various Z39.50 servers and clients available use the TCP/IP protocol to communicate between networked computers. (See Communications Protocols and TCP/IP Services earlier in the Tech Notes.) For all practical purposes, databases accessible through Z39.50 and the users who are trying to search them must both be on the same network or be connected to the Internet.

Online Catalogs and Z39.50

As integrated system vendors developed online public access catalogs (OPACs) with differing user interfaces, libraries sought ways to make it possible for patrons to search multiple catalogs without having to master multiple interfaces. The Z39.50 standard was one way to accomplish that objective. Z39.50 client software integrated into a vendor's OPAC gives an online catalog user the opportunity to search other databases from within the library's own catalog user interface. By choosing a prompt for "other databases," the OPAC user initiates a Z39.50 search without even realizing it. To the user the other databases look just like the library's own database.

A Z39.50 implementation is a classic client/server application. Client software is usually available from a library's own integrated system vendor and is imbedded into the vendor's online catalog client or user interface. If the vendor's OPAC is running on dumb terminals, the Z39.50 client software usually runs on the library's integrated system server. If the vendor has a graphical user interface (GUI) online catalog client, the Z39.50 client may run either as a part of the vendor's GUI or on the library's server.

There are also third-party Z39.50 clients (SeaChange's BookWhere? is an example), which run as standalone PC applications independent of an integrated system. These have their own user interface, which, again, are the same regardless of what systems are being searched.

The Z39.50 server is the software a Z39.50 client communicates with. The server must be developed by each integrated system or database vendor to run with its own online catalog or database. A Z39.50 server is a piece of software that translates between a vendor's internal database structure and the Z39.50 standard. The standard defines a wide variety of searches it can support, but each vendor needs to link the standard's search options to specific elements of the vendor's own database and indexes. For example, the standard defines twelve separate types of title searches that can be performed. For a vendor with only one title index, these twelve types of searches must be linked to that one index to provide reasonably complete title access.

Because the client and the server are developed by separate vendors, it is entirely possible for a library to implement only half of the Z39.50 client/server applications. A library may contract with its integrated system vendor for a Z39.50 server, which it will make available for other libraries to search, without ever adding the client functionality to its own OPAC screens. A library without an integrated system database, or with an integrated system that is not linked to the Internet, may choose to purchase only Z39.50 client software to search other libraries' databases. Just remember, you can buy clients from a number of sources, but the server has to come from the vendor who provided your database.

Cataloging and Z39.50

Although linking OPACs was the first large-scale implementation of Z39.50, it is not the only library application in which Z39.50 has proven useful. If a Z39.50 server is programmed to do so, it can send an entire MARC record to the client to satisfy a client request. Suppliers of cataloging records from the Library of Congress to commercial vendors such as The Library Corporation and Marcive have taken advantage of this feature to develop new ways for libraries to capture MARC records in machine readable form. Vendors of integrated systems are also incorporating Z39.50 client functions into their technical services client software as they develop GUI clients for their systems.

Interlibrary Loan and Z39.50

When the Z39.50 version 3 standard was expanded to include status information in the responses to inquiries, many libraries began to see Z39.50 as a potential vehicle for interlibrary loan transactions. Several vendors are basing commercial interlibrary loan applications on Z39.50's ability to search multiple databases simultaneously with a single search request, report on the status of materials, and retrieve a full MARC record. Although Z39.50 itself doesn't include any standards for managing the request and tracking functions of an interlibrary loan transaction, it can be combined with another set of standards (ISO 10160/10161) to develop a fully functioning interlibrary loan application.

World Wide Web and Z39.50

As discussed earlier, the primary impetus for the first application of Z39.50 was to make it possible to search different OPACs with a single user interface. Shortly after the first Z39.50 implementation, the World Wide Web burst onto the scene, and everyone's assumptions about user interfaces were changed forever. OPAC vendors began to develop Web interfaces for their catalogs, and the perceived problems of multiple user interfaces were greatly reduced by widespread adoption of Web OPACs.

However, every database vendor didn't develop a Web interface, and Z39.50 was never meant to be only a bibliographic record retrieval tool. It is meant to be a system-independent way to search databases. As the Web became the dominant user interface for all kinds of applications, another Z39.50-based product was born: the **Web-to-Z39.50 gateway.** This gateway is actually a piece of software that links a Z39.50 server to a Web server. Users with Web browsers connect to the Web server side of the gateway and use a Web interface to construct their search requests. The Web server interacts with the Z39.50 server to execute a Z39.50 search and receive the responses. The Web server then formats the responses as Web pages and delivers them to the inquiring browser. This makes it possible for users to query Z39.50 databases without needing to load and run Z39.50 client software.

The most important point to keep in mind is that Z39.50 services involve two separate applications: the Z39.50 server and the Z39.50 client. If you want to offer your online catalog to other libraries to be searched through Z39.50, you need to get the Z39.50 server software from your integrated system vendor. If you want to search other libraries' Z39.50 databases, or any of a number of other Z39.50-compliant databases, you need Z39.50 client software. Remember, too, that Z39.50 is a network application. You need access to the Internet to use either the server or the client features effectively.

Additional Resources

Lynch, Clifford A. "Building the Infrastructure of Resource Sharing: Union Catalogs, Distributed Search, and Cross-Database Linkage." *Library Trends* 45, no. 3 (winter 1997): 448–61.

———. "The Z39.50 Information Retrieval Standard." *D-Lib*. Apr. 1997. Online. Available at http://www.dlib.org/dlib/april97/04lynch.html. 3 Oct. 1998.

Stark, Ted. "The Net and Z39.50: Toward a Virtual Union Catalog." *Computers in Libraries* 17, no.10 (Nov./Dec. 1997): 27–9.

"Z39.50: Part 1—An Overview." *Biblio Tech Review* 26 Nov. 1997. Online. Available at http://www.biblio-tech.com/html/z39.50.html. 4 Feb. 1998.

To view a variety of vendor Z39.50 server implementations and use a Web-Z39.50 gateway go to http://lcweb.loc.gov/z3950/gateway.html#other.

A good set of Z39.50 links is maintained by the Sirsi Corporation and can be found at http://www.sirsi.com/Zresources/zlinks.html. 4 Feb. 1998.

For a more technical view, see the following sources.

Michael, James J., and Mark Hinnebusch. *From A to Z39.50: A Networking Primer.* Westport, Conn.: Mecklermedia, 1994.

Library of Congress. *Z39.50 Maintenance Agency.* 3 Feb. 1998. Online. Available at http://lcweb.loc.gov/z3950/agency/. 4 Feb. 1998.

Workforms

Tasks

Workform/Task Correlation Chart

Workform	Task															
	1	2	3	4	5	6	7	8	9	10	11	12	13	14	15	16
A	X	X	X													
B	X															
C					X											
D					X		X	X								
E					X											
F						X				X						
G						X				X						
H						X										
I							X	X	X			X	X			
J								X	X							
K									X							
L									X							
M									X		X					
N									X	X			X			
O										X				X	X	
P										X	X					
Q												X			X	X
R															X	X
S															X	
T																X

WORKFORM A **Planning Process Worksheet**

Task	Person Responsible	Others to Be Involved	Data Required	Outside Assistance	How Long
1					
2					
3					
4					
5					
6					
7					
8					

(Continued)

Copyright © 1999 American Library Association. All rights reserved. Permission granted to reproduce for nonprofit educational purposes.

WORKFORM A   **Planning Process Worksheet (cont.)**

Task	Person Responsible	Others to Be Involved	Data Required	Outside Assistance	How Long
9					
10					
11					
12					
13					
14					
15					
16					

Library _____

Completed by _____

Date _____

Copyright © 1999 American Library Association. All rights reserved. Permission granted to reproduce for nonprofit educational purposes

WORKFORM B **Planning Calendar**

Task	Jan.	Feb.	Mar.	Apr.	May	June	July	Aug.	Sept.	Oct.	Nov.	Dec.
1												
2												
3												
4												
5												
6												
7												
8												
9												
10												
11												
12												
13												
14												
15												
16												

Library _____

Completed by _____

Date _____

Copyright © 1999 American Library Association. All rights reserved. Permission granted to reproduce for nonprofit educational purposes

Goal _____ : _____

_____

_____

Objective

1 _____

_____

2 _____

_____

3 _____

_____

Activities in Plan That Have Not Been Implemented	Require Technology	Could Use Technology
1.		
2.		
3.		
4.		
5.		
6.		
7.		
8.		
9.		
10.		
Other Activities That Would Accomplish Objectives		
1.		
2.		
3.		
4.		
5.		

Completed by _____ Library _____

Date _____

Copyright © 1999 American Library Association. All rights reserved. Permission granted to reproduce for nonprofit educational purposes.

WORKFORM D   **Library Technology Needs Summary**

Instructions: In the first column, list in priority order the activities that will require or could use technology-based solutions to implement. Indicate the measure or measures of success for the activity in the second column.

Activity	Measure(s) of Success
1.	
2.	
3.	
4.	
5.	
6.	
7.	
8.	
9.	
10.	
11.	
12.	

Copyright © 1999 American Library Association. All rights reserved. Permission granted to reproduce for nonprofit educational purposes.   (Continued)

Activity	Measure(s) of Success
13.	
14.	
15.	
16.	
17.	
18.	
19.	
20.	
21.	
22.	
23.	
24.	
25.	

Completed by _____ Library _____

Date_____

Copyright © 1999 American Library Association. All rights reserved. Permission granted to reproduce for nonprofit educational purposes.

WORKFORM E Forced Choices Process

Instructions: Assign a number to each of the activities you are prioritizing. This worksheet will help you evaluate up to 15 activities against every other activity, each time determining which of your choices is the most important.

Begin in column A. Compare the first and second activities and circle the number of the one you think is most important (1 or 2). Continue through column A, then through all of the columns.

A	B	C	D	E	F	G	H	I	J	K	L	M	N
1 2	2 3	3 4	4 5	5 6	6 7	7 8	8 9	9 10	10 11	11 12	12 13	13 14	14 15
1 3	2 4	3 5	4 6	5 7	6 8	7 9	8 10	9 11	10 12	11 13	12 14	13 15	
1 4	2 5	3 6	4 7	5 8	6 9	7 10	8 11	9 12	10 13	11 14	12 15		
1 5	2 6	3 7	4 8	5 9	6 10	7 11	8 12	9 13	10 14	11 15			
1 6	2 7	3 8	4 9	5 10	6 11	7 12	8 13	9 14	10 15				
1 7	2 8	3 9	4 10	5 11	6 12	7 13	8 14	9 15					
1 8	2 9	3 10	4 11	5 12	6 13	7 14	8 15						
1 9	2 10	3 11	4 12	5 13	6 14	7 15							
1 10	2 11	3 12	4 13	5 14	6 15								
1 11	2 12	3 13	4 14	5 15									
1 12	2 13	3 14	4 15										
1 13	2 14	3 15											
1 14	2 15												
1 15													

Instructions: Count the number of times you circled each number. Place each total by the appropriate line below. Note that you must add vertically and horizontally to be sure that you include all circled choices. The item with the highest number is the one you think is most important.

1. _____
2. _____
3. _____
4. _____
5. _____
6. _____
7. _____
8. _____
9. _____
10. _____
11. _____
12. _____
13. _____
14. _____
15. _____

Completed by _____ Library _____

Date _____

Copyright © 1999 American Library Association. All rights reserved. Permission granted to reproduce for nonprofit educational purposes

Facility: _____

Part 1. Client Devices and Software

Location: _____

	Description
Client Devices	
Character-based terminal	
Protocol	
PC	
Processor type and speed	
RAM	
Disk space available	
Operating system	
Color monitor resolution	
Sound card	
Speakers or headphones	
Client Software	
IP services	
Telnet	
Browser	
Helper applications	
Application-specific client software	
Commercial applications	

Copyright © 1999 American Library Association. All rights reserved. Permission granted to reproduce for nonprofit educational purposes.

(Continued)

WORKFORM F **Current Technology Overview (cont.)**

Part 2. Servers and Printers

Facility: _____

	Number	Description
Servers		
Function:		
Processor type and speed		
RAM		
Disk space available		
Operating system		
Function:		
Processor type and speed		
RAM		
Disk space available		
Operating system		
CD server		
Number of drives		
Speed		
Other		
Printers		
Serial		
Parallel		
Networked (Y/N):		
Color (Y/N):		
Resolution		

Copyright © 1999 American Library Association. All rights reserved. Permission granted to reproduce for nonprofit educational purposes.

(Continued)

WORKFORM F **Current Technology Overview (cont.)**

Part 3. Networks

Facility: _____

	Number	Description
LAN		
Hubs		
Total ports		
Unused ports		
Network type		
Speed		
Terminal servers		
Total ports		
Unused ports		
Network type		
Speed		
Network operating system		
WAN		
Internal		
Multiplexers		
Bridges/routers		
Protocol(s) supported		
Speed		
External		
Bandwidth to ISP		

Copyright © 1999 American Library Association. All rights reserved. Permission granted to reproduce for nonprofit educational purposes.

(Continued)

WORKFORM F Current Technology Overview (cont.)

Part 4. Staff Skills

Facility: _____

Staff Skills	Number
Windows skills	
None	
Basic	
Expert	
Web-browser skills	
None	
Basic	
Expert	
Application (list): _____	
None	
Basic	
Expert	
Application (list): _____	
None	
Basic	
Expert	
Application (list): _____	
None	
Basic	
Expert	
Application (list): _____	
None	
Basic	
Expert	

Part 5. Public Skills

Facility: _____

Public Skills	Percent
Adults	
Windows skills	
None	
Basic	
Expert	
Web-browser skills	
None	
Basic	
Expert	
Children	
Windows skills	
None	
Basic	
Expert	
Web-browser skills	
None	
Basic	
Expert	

204

(Continued)

Copyright © 1999 American Library Association. All rights reserved. Permission granted to reproduce for nonprofit educational purposes.

WORKFORM F **Current Technology Overview (cont.)**

Part 6. Technical Staff Skills

TECHNICAL SKILLS	Skills Needed (Place an X in the appropriate boxes)		Skills Available (Place an X in the appropriate boxes)		Source of Additional Technical Support (if Required)
	On Staff	Available to Library	On Staff	Available to Library	
PC skills					
Install and configure hardware					
Load and update software					
Troubleshoot and repair problems					
LAN skills					
Design networks					
Install and configure hardware					
Load and update software					
Troubleshoot and repair problems					
WAN skills					
Install and configure hardware					
Load and update software					
Troubleshoot and repair problems					

Completed by _____

Date _____

Library _____

Copyright © 1999 American Library Association. All rights reserved. Permission granted to reproduce for nonprofit educational purposes

Facility: _____

Electrical

Outlets

Circuits

Cabling

Lighting

Air Conditioning

Space

Furniture (including furniture for persons with disabilities)

Completed by _____   Library _____

Date_____

Copyright © 1999 American Library Association. All rights reserved. Permission granted to reproduce for nonprofit educational purposes.

Technology Strengths

1.

2.

3.

4.

5.

Technology Weaknesses

1.

2.

3.

4.

5.

Copyright © 1999 American Library Association. All rights reserved. Permission granted to reproduce for nonprofit educational purposes.
(Continued)

Opportunities to Improve Technology

1.

2.

3.

4.

5.

Threats to Improving Technology

1.

2.

3.

4.

5.

Completed by _____ Library _____

Date_____

Copyright © 1999 American Library Association. All rights reserved. Permission granted to reproduce for nonprofit educational purposes.

Activity: _____

Product or Service: _____

General Description: _____

_____

_____

_____

Infrastructure Requirements

Workstation _____ PC _____ Other (List) _____

Network _____ LAN _____ WAN

Internet Access _____ Yes _____ No

Characteristics

Number of sites needing access _____

Number of users _____

Location(s) of users _____

Licensing restrictions _____

Frequency of updates and currency of data _____

Authentication of users _____

Indexing and retrieval features _____

User interface _____

Training requirements _____

Cost to support the product _____

Other _____

Other _____

Source(s) of Information: _____

_____

Completed by _____ Library _____

Date _____

Copyright © 1999 American Library Association. All rights reserved. Permission granted to reproduce for nonprofit educational purposes.

Instructions

1. Using the information on Workform D: Library Technology Needs Summary, write the activity that has the highest priority in the section labeled "Activity 1." Then, based on the measure(s) for the activity (found in the second column on Workform D), indicate the relative importance of each of the characteristics listed. Use the following scale:

   1. critical characteristic
   2. desirable characteristic
   3. doesn't matter

2. List the options that you identified for this activity from Workform I: Product/Service Options in the column headed "Product Review." Using the information on Workform I, rate each of the options for *each* of the characteristics. Use the following scale:

   1. option fully meets the requirements of the characteristic
   2. option partially meets the requirements of the characteristic
   3. option does not meet the requirements of the characteristic

3. Select the option that most closely matches your desired characteristics.

4. Continue in the same manner with your second and third priorities from Workform D.

Activity 1:

	Multiple Sites	Multiple Users	Frequency of Updates	Off-site Access	Currency	Indexing	Meets ADA Needs	Ease of Use	Other
Relative importance									
Product review									
Option 1:									
Option 2:									
Option 3:									
Option 4:									
Option 5:									

Characteristics

Best choice: _____

Copyright © 1999 American Library Association. All rights reserved. Permission granted to reproduce for nonprofit educational purposes.

211

(Continued)

Activity 2:

Characteristics

Product review	Multiple Sites	Multiple Users	Frequency of Updates	Off-site Access	Currency	Indexing	Meets ADA Needs	Ease of Use	Other
Relative importance									
Product review									
Option 1:									
Option 2:									
Option 3:									
Option 4:									
Option 5:									

Best choice: _____

Activity 3:

Characteristics

Product review	Multiple Sites	Multiple Users	Frequency of Updates	Off-site Access	Currency	Indexing	Meets ADA Needs	Ease of Use	Other
Relative importance									
Product review									
Option 1:									
Option 2:									
Option 3:									
Option 4:									
Option 5:									

Best choice: _____

Library _____

Completed by _____

Date _____

Copyright © 1999 American Library Association. All rights reserved. Permission granted to reproduce for nonprofit educational purposes

Option # _____ :

Part 1. **Client Devices and Software**

	Description		Number Needed	Cost per Unit	Total Cost
Client Devices					
Character-based terminal	Yes	No			
If yes, protocol needed					
PC	Yes	No			
Processor type and speed					
RAM					
Disk space needed					
Operating system					
Color monitor or graphics card	Yes	No			
If yes, requirement					
Sound card	Yes	No			
If yes, type					
Speakers or headphones	Yes	No			
Speech synthesizer	Yes	No			
Adaptive keyboard	Yes	No			
Client Software					
Application software (list)					
Telnet					
Browser					
Helper applications (list)					

(Continued)

Copyright © 1999 American Library Association. All rights reserved. Permission granted to reproduce for nonprofit educational purposes.

Other software (list)			

Part 2. Servers and Printers

Description	Number Needed	Cost per Unit	Total Cost
Servers			
Function: _____			
Processor type and speed			
RAM			
Disk space needed			
Operating system			
CD server Yes No			
Number of drives			
Speed			
Other requirements (list)			
Printers			
Networked Yes No			
Serial or parallel			
Color			
Resolution			
Individual workstation printers Yes No			
Serial or parallel			
Color			
Resolution			

Copyright © 1999 American Library Association. All rights reserved. Permission granted to reproduce for nonprofit educational purposes.

(Continued)

WORKFORM K   Infrastructure Evaluation (cont.)

Part 3. Networks

Description	Number Needed	Cost per Unit	Total Cost
LAN			
Type			
Speed			
Hubs/switches			
Speed			
Terminal servers			
Terminal protocol			
Speed			
WAN			
Internal			
Communication links			
Bandwidth of links			
Routers/bridges			
Type			
Protocol(s) supported			
Resolution			
External			
Number of links and bandwidth to ISP			
ISP services			

Copyright © 1999 American Library Association. All rights reserved. Permission granted to reproduce for nonprofit educational purposes.

(Continued)

WORKFORM K **Infrastructure Evaluation (cont.)**

Part 4. Staff Skills

Level of Skill Needed	Current Skill Level of Staff Users	Number of Staff Needing Training
Staff: _____		
Windows skills		
None		
Basic		
Expert		
Web-browser skills		
None		
Basic		
Expert		
Application-specific skills		
None		
Basic		
Expert		
Commercial-application skills		
Application: _____		
None		
Basic		
Expert		
Application: _____		
None		
Basic		
Expert		
Application: _____		
None		
Basic		
Expert		

Copyright © 1999 American Library Association. All rights reserved. Permission granted to reproduce for nonprofit educational purposes.

(Continued)

Part 5. Public Skills

Level of Skill Needed	Percentage Estimate of Current Skill Level	Percentage of Public Needing Training
Windows skills		
None		
Basic		
Expert		
Web-browser skills		
None		
Basic		
Expert		
Application-specific skills		
Application: _____		
None		
Basic		
Expert		
Application: _____		
None		
Basic		
Expert		
Application: _____		
None		
Basic		
Expert		

Copyright © 1999 American Library Association. All rights reserved. Permission granted to reproduce for nonprofit educational purposes.

(Continued)

217

Part 6. Technical Skills

	Skills Needed (Place an X in the appropriate boxes)		Skills Available (Place an X in the appropriate boxes)		Source of Additional Technical Support (if Required)
	Yes	**No**	**On Staff**	**Available to Library**	
PC skills					
Install and configure hardware					
Load and update software					
Troubleshoot and repair problems					
LAN skills					
Design networks					
Install and configure hardware					
Load and update software					
Troubleshoot and repair problems					
WAN skills					
Install and configure hardware					
Load and update software					
Troubleshoot and repair problems					

Completed by _____

Date _____

Library _____

Copyright © 1999 American Library Association. All rights reserved. Permission granted to reproduce for nonprofit educational purposes

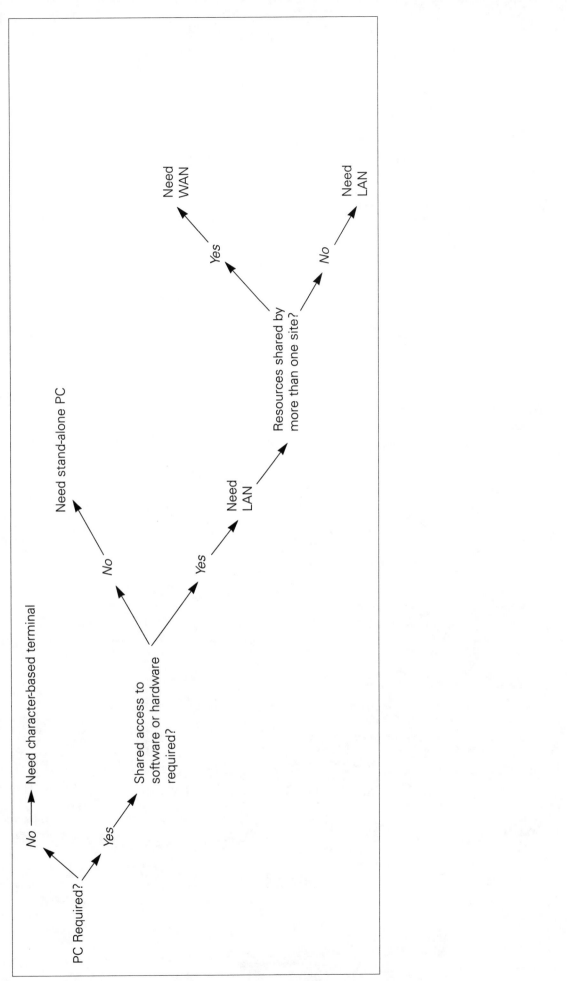

PC Required?

No → Need character-based terminal

Yes → Shared access to software or hardware required?

No → Need stand-alone PC

Yes → Need LAN → Resources shared by more than one site?

Yes → Need WAN

No → Need LAN

Completed by _____

Date _____

Library _____

Copyright © 1999 American Library Association. All rights reserved. Permission granted to reproduce for nonprofit educational purposes

WORKFORM M Infrastructure Requirements Comparison

Part 1. Equipment Required

	Option 1		Option 2		Option 3		Proposed Infrastructure	
Client Devices								
Character-based terminal	Yes	No	Yes	No	Yes	No	Yes	No
Protocol required								
PC	Yes	No	Yes	No	Yes	No	Yes	No
Servers								
Function: _____	Yes	No	Yes	No	Yes	No	Yes	No
Function: _____	Yes	No	Yes	No	Yes	No	Yes	No
Function: _____	Yes	No	Yes	No	Yes	No	Yes	No
CD Server	Yes	No	Yes	No	Yes	No	Yes	No
Other: _____	Yes	No	Yes	No	Yes	No	Yes	No
Printers								
Individual	Yes	No	Yes	No	Yes	No	Yes	No
Networked	Yes	No	Yes	No	Yes	No	Yes	No

Copyright © 1999 American Library Association. All rights reserved. Permission granted to reproduce for nonprofit educational purposes.

(Continued)

Part 2. Software Required

	Option 1		Option 2		Option 3		Proposed Infrastructure	
Operating Systems								
End user devices								
Server								
Client Software								
Application software (list)								
	Yes	No	Yes	No	Yes	No	Yes	No
	Yes	No	Yes	No	Yes	No	Yes	No
Telnet	Yes	No	Yes	No	Yes	No	Yes	No
Browser	Yes	No	Yes	No	Yes	No	Yes	No
Other client software	Yes	No	Yes	No	Yes	No	Yes	No

Copyright © 1999 American Library Association. All rights reserved. Permission granted to reproduce for nonprofit educational purposes.

(Continued)

Part 3. Networks Required

	Option 1		Option 2		Option 3		Proposed Infrastructure	
	Yes	No	Yes	No	Yes	No	Yes	No
LAN	Yes	No	Yes	No	Yes	No	Yes	No
If Yes, list locations below								
WAN								
Internal	Yes	No	Yes	No	Yes	No	Yes	No
If Yes, list locations below								
External	Yes	No	Yes	No	Yes	No	Yes	No
If Yes, list locations below								
Connection to ISP	Yes	No	Yes	No	Yes	No	Yes	No

(Continued)

Copyright © 1999 American Library Association. All rights reserved. Permission granted to reproduce for nonprofit educational purposes.

WORKFORM M Infrastructure Requirements Comparison (cont.)

Part 4. Staff Skills

	Option 1		Option 2		Option 3		Proposed Infrastructure	
Windows skills	Yes	No	Yes	No	Yes	No	Yes	No
Web-browser skills	Yes	No	Yes	No	Yes	No	Yes	No
Application-specific skills (list)								
	Yes	No	Yes	No	Yes	No	Yes	No
	Yes	No	Yes	No	Yes	No	Yes	No
Commercial-application skills (list)								
	Yes	No	Yes	No	Yes	No	Yes	No
	Yes	No	Yes	No	Yes	No	Yes	No

Part 5. Public Skills

	Option 1		Option 2		Option 3		Proposed Infrastructure	
Windows skills	Yes	No	Yes	No	Yes	No	Yes	No
Web-browser skills	Yes	No	Yes	No	Yes	No	Yes	No
Application-specific skills (list)								
	Yes	No	Yes	No	Yes	No	Yes	No
	Yes	No	Yes	No	Yes	No	Yes	No

Copyright © 1999 American Library Association. All rights reserved. Permission granted to reproduce for nonprofit educational purposes.

(Continued)

WORKFORM M   **Infrastructure Requirements Comparison (cont.)**

Part 6. Technical Skills

	Option 1		Option 2		Option 3		Proposed Infrastructure	
PC skills								
Install and configure hardware	Yes	No	Yes	No	Yes	No	Yes	No
Load and update software	Yes	No	Yes	No	Yes	No	Yes	No
Troubleshoot and repair problems	Yes	No	Yes	No	Yes	No	Yes	No
LAN skills								
Design networks	Yes	No	Yes	No	Yes	No	Yes	No
Install and configure hardware	Yes	No	Yes	No	Yes	No	Yes	No
Load and update software	Yes	No	Yes	No	Yes	No	Yes	No
Troubleshoot and repair problems	Yes	No	Yes	No	Yes	No	Yes	No
WAN skills								
Install and configure hardware	Yes	No	Yes	No	Yes	No	Yes	No
Load and update software	Yes	No	Yes	No	Yes	No	Yes	No
Troubleshoot and repair problems	Yes	No	Yes	No	Yes	No	Yes	No

Completed by _____

Date _____

Library _____

Copyright © 1999 American Library Association. All rights reserved. Permission granted to reproduce for nonprofit educational purposes

Character-Based Terminals	Have	Need	Gap
Protocol required:			

Plan for Filling Gap or Reallocating Surplus

(Continued)

Copyright © 1999 American Library Association. All rights reserved. Permission granted to reproduce for nonprofit educational purposes.

PCs	Have	Need	Gap
Processor type and speed:			
RAM:			
Hard drive space:			
Operating system:			
Color monitor (Y/N):			
Speech synthesizer (Y/N):			
Adaptive keyboard (Y/N):			
Sound card (Y/N):			
Speakers or headphones: (Y/N):			

Plan for Filling Gap or Reallocating Surplus

Copyright © 1999 American Library Association. All rights reserved. Permission granted to reproduce for nonprofit educational purposes.

(Continued)

Servers	Have	Need	Gap
Processor type and speed			
RAM:			
Disk space needed			
Operating system			
CD server (Y/N):			
Number of drives			
Speed			
Other			

Plan for Filling Gap or Reallocating Surplus

Copyright © 1999 American Library Association. All rights reserved. Permission granted to reproduce for nonprofit educational purposes.

(Continued)

WORKFORM N **Gap Analysis (cont.)**

Printers	Have	Need	Gap
Individual workstation printers			
Color (Y/N):			
Resolution			
Networked printers (Y/N):			
Color (Y/N):			
Resolution			

Plan for Filling Gap or Reallocating Surplus

Copyright © 1999 American Library Association. All rights reserved. Permission granted to reproduce for nonprofit educational purposes.

(Continued)

LAN by Location	Have	Need	Gap
Location: _____			
Hubs/switches			
Protocol			
Speed			
Terminal servers			
Protocol			
Speed			

Plan for Filling Gap or Reallocating Surplus

Copyright © 1999 American Library Association. All rights reserved. Permission granted to reproduce for nonprofit educational purposes.

(Continued)

WAN by Location	Have	Need	Gap
Location: _____			
Internal			
Routers/bridges			
Protocol(s) supported			
Terminal servers			
Protocol			
Speed			
External			
Bandwidth to ISP			

Plan for Filling Gap or Reallocating Surplus

Copyright © 1999 American Library Association. All rights reserved. Permission granted to reproduce for nonprofit educational purposes.

(Continued)

Staff Skills	Have	Need	Gap
Windows			
None			
Basic			
Expert			
Web			
None			
Basic			
Expert			
Application specific: _____			
None			
Basic			
Expert			
Commercial application: _____			
None			
Basic			
Expert			

Plan for Filling Gap or Reallocating Surplus

Copyright © 1999 American Library Association. All rights reserved. Permission granted to reproduce for nonprofit educational purposes.

(Continued)

Public Skills	Have	Need	Gap
Windows			
None			
Basic			
Expert			
Web			
None			
Basic			
Expert			
Application specific: _____			
None			
Basic			
Expert			

Plan for Filling Gap or Reallocating Surplus

Copyright © 1999 American Library Association. All rights reserved. Permission granted to reproduce for nonprofit educational purposes.

(Continued)

WORKFORM N **Gap Analysis (cont.)**

Technical Skills	Have	Need	Gap
PC skills			
Install and configure hardware			
Load and update software			
Troubleshoot and repair problems			
LAN skills			
Design networks			
Install and configure hardware			
Load and update software			
Troubleshoot and repair problems			
WAN skills			
Install and configure hardware			
Load and update software			
Troubleshoot and repair problems			
Plan for Filling Gap or Reallocating Surplus			

Completed by _____

Date _____

Library _____

Copyright © 1999 American Library Association. All rights reserved. Permission granted to reproduce for nonprofit educational purposes

WORKFORM O **Summary of Investments Needed for Proposed Infrastructure**

Part 1. Equipment Required

Description	Number Needed	Cost per Unit	Total Cost
Client Devices			
Character-based terminal			
PC			
Processor			
RAM			
Hard drive			
Operating system			
Color monitor			
Speech synthesizer			
Adaptive keyboard			
Sound card			
Speakers			
Headphones			
Servers			
Function:			
Processor			
RAM			
Disk space			
Operating system			
CD server			
Number of drives			
Speed			
Other			

(Continued)

Copyright © 1999 American Library Association. All rights reserved. Permission granted to reproduce for nonprofit educational purposes.

WORKFORM O **Summary of Investments Needed for Proposed Infrastructure (cont.)**

Description	Number Needed	Cost per Unit	Total Cost
Printers			
Individual			
Serial			
Parallel			
Networked			
Serial			
Parallel			

Part 2. Software Required

Description	Number Needed	Cost per Unit	Total Cost
Client Software			
Application software (list)			
Telnet			
Browser			
Helper applications (list)			
Other software (list)			

Copyright © 1999 American Library Association. All rights reserved. Permission granted to reproduce for nonprofit educational purposes.

(Continued)

WORKFORM O **Summary of Investments Needed for Proposed Infrastructure (cont.)**

Part 3. Networks Required

Description	Number Needed	Cost per Unit	Total Cost
LAN			
Hubs			
Terminal servers			
WAN			
Internal			
Communications links			
Routers/bridges			
Terminal servers			
External			
Telecommunications suppliers			
ISP services			

Part 4. Staff Skills

Description	Number to Train	Time Needed per Person	Average Cost per Hour	Total Cost per Person
Windows skills				
Web-browser skills				
Application-specific skills				
Commercial-application skills				

Copyright © 1999 American Library Association. All rights reserved. Permission granted to reproduce for nonprofit educational purposes.

(Continued)

WORKFORM O Summary of Investments Needed for Proposed Infrastructure (cont.)

Part 5. Public Skills

	Number to Train	Description	Time Needed per Person	Average Cost per Hour	Total Cost per Person
Windows skills					
Web-browser skills					
Application-specific skills					

Part 6. Technical Skills

	Number to Train	Description	Time Needed per Person	Average Cost per Hour	Total Cost per Person
PC skills					
Install and configure hardware					
Load and update software					
Troubleshoot and repair problems					
LAN skills					
Design networks					
Install and configure hardware					
Load and update software					
Troubleshoot and repair problems					
WAN skills					
Install and configure hardware					
Load and update software					
Troubleshoot and repair problems					

Copyright © 1999 American Library Association. All rights reserved. Permission granted to reproduce for nonprofit educational purposes.

(Continued)

WORKFORM O **Summary of Investments Needed for Proposed Infrastructure (cont.)**

Part 7. Facility Upgrades

	Upgrade Needed	Estimated Cost
Electrical		
Circuits		
Outlets		
Cabling		
Lighting		
Air Conditioning		
Space		
Furniture (including furniture for persons with disabilities)		

Completed by _____

Date _____

Library _____

Copyright © 1999 American Library Association. All rights reserved. Permission granted to reproduce for nonprofit educational purposes

WORKFORM P Summary of Purchase and Ongoing Costs

Part 1. Equipment Required

	One-Time Costs		Annual Costs		
	Purchase	Installation	Maintenance	Amortization Allowance	Support
Client Devices					
Character-based terminal					
PC					
New					
Upgrades					
Color monitor					
Speech synthesizer					
Adaptive keyboard					
Sound card					
Speakers					
Headphones					
Servers					
New					
Upgrade					
CD server					
Other					
Printers					
Individual					
Network					
Subtotal					

(Continued)

Copyright © 1999 American Library Association. All rights reserved. Permission granted to reproduce for nonprofit educational purposes.

Part 2. Software Required

	One-Time Costs			Annual Costs	
	Purchase	Installation	Maintenance	Amortization Allowance	Support
Client Software					
Telnet					
Browser					
Helper applications (list)					
Other client software (list)					
Other applications (list)					
Subtotal					

Copyright © 1999 American Library Association. All rights reserved. Permission granted to reproduce for nonprofit educational purposes.

(Continued)

WORKFORM P Summary of Purchase and Ongoing Costs (cont.)

Part 3. Networks Required

	One-Time Costs		Annual Costs		
	Purchase	Installation	Maintenance	Amortization Allowance	Support
LAN					
Equipment					
Site preparation					
WAN					
Internal					
Equipment					
Phone lines					
External					
Phone line					
ISP services					
Subtotal					

Part 4. Staff Skills

	Initial Requirements			Annual Requirements		
	Number to Train	Cost Per Person	Total Cost	Number to Train	Cost Per Person	Total Cost
Window skills						
Web-browser skills						
Application: _____						
Application: _____						
Application: _____						
Subtotal						

Copyright © 1999 American Library Association. All rights reserved. Permission granted to reproduce for nonprofit educational purposes.

(Continued)

WORKFORM P Summary of Purchase and Ongoing Costs (cont.)

Part 5. Public Skills

	Initial Requirements			Annual Requirements		
	Number to Train	Cost Per Person	Total Cost	Number to Train	Cost Per Person	Total Cost
Window skills						
Web-browser skills						
Application: _____						
Application: _____						
Application: _____						
Subtotal						

Part 6. Technical Administration Skills

	Initial Requirements			Annual Requirements		
	Number to Train	Cost Per Person	Total Cost	Number to Train	Cost Per Person	Total Cost
PC skills						
Install and configure hardware						
Load and update software						
Troubleshoot and repair problems						
LAN skills						
Design networks						
Install and configure hardware						
Load and update software						
Troubleshoot and repair problems						
WAN skills						
Install and configure hardware						
Load and update software						
Troubleshoot and repair problems						
Subtotal						

Copyright © 1999 American Library Association. All rights reserved. Permission granted to reproduce for nonprofit educational purposes.

(Continued)

WORKFORM P Summary of Purchase and Ongoing Costs (cont.)

Part 7. Facility Upgrades

	Initial Cost to Upgrade	Annual Cost to Maintain
Electrical		
Circuits		
Outlets		
Cabling		
Lighting		
Air Conditioning		
Space		
Furniture (including furniture for persons with disabilities)		
Subtotal		

(Continued)

Copyright © 1999 American Library Association. All rights reserved. Permission granted to reproduce for nonprofit educational purposes.

WORKFORM P **Summary of Purchase and Ongoing Costs (cont.)**

Part 8. Summary of Costs/Requirements

	One-Time Costs or Initial Requirements/Costs	Annual Costs/ Requirements
1. Equipment		
2. Client Software		
3. Networks		
4. Staff Skill Training		
5. Public Skill Training		
6. Technical Skill Training		
7. Facility Upgrades		
Grand Total		

Completed by _____

Date _____

Library _____

Copyright © 1999 American Library Association. All rights reserved. Permission granted to reproduce for nonprofit educational purposes

Instructions: In the first column, copy the activities that will require or could use technology-based solutions to implement from Workform I: Product/ Service Options. In the second column, write the product or service that you have selected to support that activity.

Activity	Selected Product or Service
1.	
2.	
3.	
4.	
5.	
6.	
7.	
8.	
9.	
10.	
11.	
12.	

Copyright © 1999 American Library Association. All rights reserved. Permission granted to reproduce for nonprofit educational purposes.   (Continued)

Activity	Selected Product or Service
13.	
14.	
15.	
16.	
17.	
18.	
19.	
20.	
21.	
22.	
23.	
24.	
25.	

Completed by _____ Library _____

Date_____

Copyright © 1999 American Library Association. All rights reserved. Permission granted to reproduce for nonprofit educational purposes.

Stage #_____: [describe]

Beginning Date: _____ **Completion Date:** _____

Activities in Stage # _____		Person(s) Responsible	Start/End Date	Prerequisite Activities
1.				
2.				
3.				
4.				
5.				
6.				
7.				
8,				
9.				
10.				
11.				
12				
13.				
14.				

Completed by _____ Library _____

Date _____

Copyright © 1999 American Library Association. All rights reserved. Permission granted to reproduce for nonprofit educational purposes.

251

WORKFORM S **Technology Plan Implementation Time Line**

Phase ___ : [describe] _____

Activities	Jan.	Feb.	Mar.	Apr.	May	June	July	Aug.	Sept.	Oct.	Nov.	Dec.

Library _____

Completed by _____

Date _____

Copyright © 1999 American Library Association. All rights reserved. Permission granted to reproduce for nonprofit educational purposes

Stage: _____

Activity: _____

Trigger-Point Decision: _____

Assumptions:

1. _____
   _____
   _____
   _____
   _____
   _____
   _____

2. _____
   _____
   _____
   _____
   _____
   _____

3. _____
   _____
   _____
   _____
   _____
   _____
   _____

4. _____
   _____
   _____
   _____
   _____
   _____
   _____

5. _____
   _____
   _____
   _____
   _____
   _____
   _____

Completed by _____ Library _____

Date _____

Copyright © 1999 American Library Association. All rights reserved. Permission granted to reproduce for nonprofit educational purposes.

Index